Freedom and the Court

CIVIL RIGHTS AND LIBERTIES IN THE UNITED STATES

Freedom and the Court

CIVIL RIGHTS AND LIBERTIES
IN THE UNITED STATES

FOURTH EDITION

HENRY J. ABRAHAM

JAMES HART PROFESSOR OF
GOVERNMENT AND FOREIGN AFFAIRS
UNIVERSITY OF VIRGINIA

New York · *Oxford*
OXFORD UNIVERSITY PRESS
1982

Copyright © 1967, 1972, 1977, 1982 by Oxford University Press, Inc.

Library of Congress Cataloging in Publication Data

Abraham, Henry Julian, 1921–
Freedom and the Court.

Bibliography: p.
Includes indexes.
1. Civil rights—United States.   2. United States.
Supreme Court.   I. Title.
KF4749.A73   1982   342.73′085   81-745
ISBN 0-19-502960-7   AACR2
ISBN 0-19-502961-5 (pbk.)

Printing (last digit): 9 8 7 6 5 4 3

Printed in the United States of America

TO

MY MOTHER

AND

THE MEMORY OF MY FATHER

Preface to the Fourth Edition

Although the four-and-a-half years that have elapsed since the publication of this work's third edition had brought only one change in the membership of the Supreme Court of the United States—the appointment of Sandra Day O'Connor as of the fall term 1981—far-reaching, indeed seminal, changes informed the Court's interpretations and molding of constitutional law between 1977 and 1981. These developments have brushed or embraced all components and segments of that law; but none has seen such extensive, indeed, dramatic, perhaps even radical, extension or transformation as the "equal protection of the laws" realm of the Fourteenth Amendment, with particular reference to race and gender. This new (fourth) edition of the book, which has continued to be used widely and approvingly, takes account of these and other fundamental alterations in the status of civil rights and liberties in our land, as pronounced by its highest tribunal. Completely updated and thoroughly rewritten, this latest edition is current through the Court's entire 1980–81 term (ending in July of 1981), thus taking account of contemporary holdings of the "Burger Court."

Once again I happily acknowledge the profound debt I owe to a host of colleagues and students whose constructive criticism, aid, and counsel have been as welcome as they have been indispensable. Their encouragement and support are responsible for the present undertaking. I am also deeply grateful for financial research assistance tendered so generously by the Joseph and Rebecca Mitchell Foundation and the Robert W. and Patricia T. Gelfman Fund. A special note of recognition and appreciation goes to my 1979–81 research assistants, Peter M. Dodson, Linda McClain, and Vincent M. Bonventre, whose conscientious, efficient, and loyal labors were essential to the enterprise.

Charlottesville, Virginia　　　　　　　　　　　　　　　　　　　　H.J.A.
September 1981

Preface to the Third Edition

The favorable reception accorded to the first and second editions of this book prompted the undertaking of this third. Although the scope and approach of the new work are the same as that of its predecessors, the passage of time—however brief in the annals of constitutional development—has mandated changes, often major, on almost every page, indeed the rewriting as well as enlarging of most chapters. The new edition has been completely updated through 1976, thus taking account of the latest posture of the "Burger Court."

Again, I am profoundly grateful to the numerous colleagues and students whose thoughtfully constructive criticism and support of the first and second editions encouraged me to undertake the third. And I should like to add a special note of gratitude to my 1974–76 research assistant, Bruce Allen Murphy, whose superb, faithful work was essential to the revision's completion.

Keswick, Virginia   H.J.A.
January 1977

Preface to the Second Edition

The favorable reception accorded to the first edition of this book prompted the undertaking of this second, which appears almost five years later. Although the scope and approach of the new work are the same as that of the original, the passage of time—however brief in the annals of constitutional development—has mandated changes on almost every page and the rewriting as well as enlarging of certain chapters, particularly IV, V, VI, and VII. The new edition has been completely updated through December 1971, thus taking account of the latest posture of the "Burger Court." There are two procedural innovations: the addition of an appendix containing excerpts from the Constitution dealing with civil rights and liberties, and a separate "name" index (alongside "general" and "case" indexes).

I am profoundly grateful to the numerous colleagues and students whose thoughtfully constructive criticism and support of the first edition encouraged me to undertake the second. And I should like to add a special note of gratitude to my 1970–72 research assistants, Norman H. Levine, Mark A. Aronchick, Frank C. Lindgren, Andrew B. Cohn, and Michael E. Marino.

Wynnewood, Pennsylvania   H.J.A.
February 1972

Preface to the First Edition

This is essentially a study of the lines that must be drawn by a democratic society as it attempts to reconcile individual freedom with the rights of the community. No single book could cope with the entire field of civil rights and liberties, and no attempt is made to do so here. Rather, it has been my aim to analyze and evaluate the basic problem of drawing lines between individual rights and community rights and to venture some conclusions or suggestions in those spheres that constitute the basic rights and liberties: freedom of religion and the attendant problem of separation of Church and State; freedom of expression; due process of law, particularly procedural safeguards in criminal law; and political and racial equality. The three introductory chapters—the third comprising a thorough analysis of the problem of Amendment Fourteen and "incorporation"—are designed to focus the study and to stress my belief that it is essential to recognize and comprehend the significant role the judicial branch of the United States Government, with the Supreme Court as its apex, has played in defining and strengthening the basic rights and liberties that accrue to us from the principle of a government under constitutionalism, a government that is limited in its impact upon individual freedom.

As usual, I am indebted to many colleagues for stimulation, criticism, and encouragement. I am particularly grateful to Professor Alpheus T. Mason of Princeton who read the entire manuscript; to Professors David Fellman of Wisconsin and Rocco J. Tresolini of Lehigh who were generous discussants; and to my departmental colleague, Charles Jasper Cooper, who proved a valued "sounding board" down the hall. My research assistant, Judy F. Lang, was a delightful and industrious aid. Dr. Joan I. Gotwals of the Van Pelt Library kindly provided me with a "secret annex" in which I could work in quiet seclusion. Mrs. Dorothy E. Carpenter typed the manuscript cheerfully and conscientiously. Byron S. Hollinshead, Jr.,

Helen M. Richardson, and Mary Ollmann of Oxford University Press provided indispensable professional assistance. And my wife Mildred and our sons Philip and Peter, to each of whom earlier books were happily dedicated, made it all worthwhile.

Wynnewood, Pennsylvania   H.J.A.
March 1967

on Civil Rights, which became a busy and assertive unit in the governmental struggle against racial discrimination. A second transformed the small and weak Civil Rights Section in the Department of Justice into the more effective Civil Rights Division, headed by an Assistant Attorney-General. A third and fourth not only authorized the federal government to obtain federal civil injunctions against actual or threatened interference with the right to vote (with or without the individual's consent) and to pay the costs for the litigation but also gave the appropriate United States District Courts jurisdiction over such suits without the normal requirement that all state judicial and administrative remedies be first "exhausted below."

Civil Rights Act of 1960. Despite considerable activity by the new Civil Rights Commission, however, the 1957 statute proved to be of only marginal value. Nevertheless, it served to focus and popularize aspects of the problem; and its weaknesses did prompt the Eisenhower Administration to call for a new statute, which became the Civil Rights Act of 1960. No longer did the Southern members of Congress have the necessary number of votes and allies to block such measures. The Act of 1960 promised to be a far-reaching piece of legislation chiefly because, in an elaborate provision for appointment of federal "voting referees," it undertook to safeguard the black citizen's right to vote freely and without discrimination. The measure authorized federal district courts, through appointment of these referees, to enroll qualified voters for *all* state as well as federal elections in areas where local officials systematically denied them the right to register or to vote. And it enabled the federal Department of Justice to file suit to bring about this desired result. More than fifteen times as many suits were brought during the Act of 1960's first three years of life than had been brought during any similar span of time under the previous statute.

Still, black leaders and other civil rights spokesmen regarded the Act of 1960 as too slow, too costly to administer, and too cumbersome. Black restlessness and impatience—assuredly understandable if not inevitably justifiable in all instances—were intensified; the year 1963 saw the peak of visible public protest movements. Reiterating their "loss of faith in the white power structure," blacks took to the streets in ever-increasing numbers throughout the United States. The summer of 1963 became known as the "long, hot summer," culminating late in August in a massive, peaceful, interracial march by some 20,000 people in Washington, D.C., billed as the "March on Washington for Jobs and Freedom." Other demonstrations were not so peaceful and orderly, especially some of those that took place in scattered cities in the deep South where feelings ran high. Although not necessarily directly connected with the demonstrations, reprisals by white extremists resulted in forty-four violent deaths during 1963, 1964, and

1965.[156] The black riots in Northern cities in the summer of 1966 led to a score more. Against this background of mounting anger, threats, and sporadic violence, President Kennedy had asked Congress twice in 1963 for new, strong, and expanded civil rights legislation. President Johnson again requested it when he first addressed Congress as the nation's new Chief Executive following the tragic assassination of President Kennedy on November 22. In the following June, Congress passed the Civil Rights Act of 1964.

Civil Rights Act of 1964. Demonstrably, that statute was the most comprehensive piece of legislation to be enacted by the federal legislature since the ill-fated measures of the 1870s. It cleared the House with relative ease, 290:130. But its success in the Senate, by a bi-partisan vote of 73:27, was delayed until the breaking of a 75-day Southern filibuster by the application of the Senate's debate-limiting cloture rule on the eighty-third day of debate by a vote of 71:29.[157] It was the first time that cloture had been attained on a civil rights filibuster since the adoption of the cloture rule in 1917.

The principal provisions of the Civil Rights Act of 1964:

extended the heretofore sharply limited life of the Civil Rights Commission for four years, to 1968 (extended periodically since then), and broadened both its duties and powers;

established a Community Relations Service to aid in the conciliation of racial disputes;

forbade, in its crucial Title VII, discrimination because of race, color, sex, religion, or national origin either by employers or by labor unions in business concerns with 100 employees or more, this number to drop by stages to 25 by 1968,[158]—public employees were covered as of a 1972 amend-

[156] *The Southern Regional Council Report,* released on January 30, 1966. Among these murders were those of Mississippi NAACP leader Medgar Evers near his Jackson home; a pro-civil rights white Baltimore postman, William L. Moore, in northeast Alabama; the bomb-murder of four 11- to 14-year-old Negro girls in the 16th Street Birmingham Baptist church (eleven years later, Chris McNair, the father of one of the murdered girls, was elected chairman of the Jefferson County—Birmingham—delegation to the Alabama House of Representatives); and, almost on the day of the passage of the 1964 Act, the murder of three young civil rights workers, two white and one black, near Philadelphia, Mississippi. According to the S.R.C.'s report, eighty civil rights murders were committed between 1956 and 1966.

[157] On the bill's final roll call, 46 Democrats and 27 Republicans voted in favor of it; 21 Democrats and 6 Republicans against. Voting to invoke cloture were 44 Democrats and 27 Republicans; opposed were 23 Democrats and 6 Republicans.

[158] In the first interpretation of this provision as it relates to racial bias, the Supreme Court ruled 8:0 in March 1971 that it bars job tests by employers that screen out blacks without realistically measuring their qualifications to do the work. (*Griggs v. Duke Power Co.,* 401 U.S. 424.) On the other hand, the Court ruled 7:2 five years later, in the absence of proof of "racially discriminatory purpose," a statute

ment—and created an Equal Economic Opportunity Commission (E.E.O.C.) to administer that aspect of the Act;

prohibited voting registrars from applying different standards to white and black applicants, required all literacy tests to be in writing, and rendered a sixth-grade education a "rebuttable assumption" of literacy;[159]

permitted the Attorney-General to bring suit, upon written complaint by aggrieved individuals, to secure desegregation of facilities owned, operated, or managed by state and local governments;

authorized, in its tough Title VI, the executive to halt any federal aid funds to either public or private programs "or activities" in which racial discrimination on grounds of race, color, or national origin[160]—note that "religion" is not included; it *is* in Title VII—is allowed to continue (a provision used since with considerable success—and increasingly accompanied by serious, and not inevitably rebuttable, charges of "preferential treatment" and *"reverse* discrimination"[161]—by the Departments of Labor, Health and Human Services, and Education,[162] coupled with Title IV grants available

---

or an official act is *not* unconstitutional just because it places a "substantially disproportionate" burden on one race. (*Washington v. Davis,* 426 U.S. 229 [1976] involving a written qualifying test for members of the District of Columbia Police Department.) Also, the Court refused to review an unsuccessful challenge by blacks of the Georgia bar exam, which blacks had traditionally failed in greater numbers than whites. (*Tyler v. Vickey,* 426 U.S. 940 [1976].) Just prior to the end of its 1975–76 term, the Supreme Court held 7:2 and 9:0, in opinions written by its only black member, Mr. Justice Marshall, that §1981 of the Civil Rights Act of 1866 as well as Title VII of that of 1964 prohibit employers from discrimination against whites on the basis of their race in and to the same extent they prohibit racial discrimination against blacks. (*McDonald v. Santa Fe Transportation Co.,* 427 U.S. 273 [1976].) And in 1978 it upheld 5:2 the use of the National Teacher Examination Test to determine hiring and promotion in a state, although the test results disqualified more than four times as many blacks as whites. (*National Education Association v. South Carolina,* 434 U.S. 1026.) See also the related, unanimous 1981 decision in *Texas Department of Community Affairs v. Burdine,* 49 LW 4214.

[159] See pp. 360 ff. for pertinent changes effected by the Voting Rights Act of 1965, amended and extended in 1970 and 1975.

[160] Broadly interpreted by the Department of Health, Education, and Welfare, for example, to *require* special assistance to non-English-speaking Chinese students—who were far from eager for such help—with the Court upholding the requirement in a multiple-opinion decision in 1974. (*Lau v. Nichols,* 414 U.S. 563.)

[161] E.g., see Mr. Justice Douglas's remarkable dissenting opinion in *De Funis v. Odegaard,* 417 U.S. 623, 1974—the University of Washington "reverse discrimination" case, in which a majority of five ducked the delicate issue by ruling the case "moot." Douglas wrote there: "The Equal Protection Clause commands the elimination of racial barriers, not their creation in order to satisfy our theory as to how society ought to be organized." (*De Funis,* at 342.) See also Mary K. Hammond, "May the Constitution be Color Conscious to Remain Color Blind?," I *Ohio Northern University Law Review* 81 (1973) and the extensive discussion of the "reverse discrimination" issue in connection with the *Bakke, Weber,* and *Fullilove* decisions, *infra,* pp. 396 ff.

[162] Until 1980 the latter two were part and parcel of the erstwhile Department of Health, Education, and Welfare.

to state and local agencies to help them cope with problems stemming from school desegregation);

outlawed, in its Public Accommodation Title II, discrimination because of race, religion, color, or national origin in hotels, restaurants, theaters, gas stations, and all other public accommodations that affect interstate commerce, as well as in all public facilities (Title II was specifically held constitutional in December 1964, the first test of any provision of the Act of 1964 to reach the United States Supreme Court);[163] and

empowered the Attorney-General to file enforcement suits against any owners of public accommodations who discriminate, and on behalf of any persons whose constitutional rights are deemed violated in school segregation or other instances.[164]

Understandably, the two most controversial provisions of the Civil Rights Act of 1964, both prior to and during the national debate that attended its conception and birth, were the two then most obviously concerned with delicate "line-drawing": those dealing with fair employment practices[165]

---

[163] *Heart of Atlanta Motel v. United States*, 379 U.S. 241 and *Katzenbach v. McClung*, 379 U.S. 294. Mr. Justice Clark's opinion for the unanimous Court rested the case for Title II's constitutionality on the congressional power over interstate commerce—although Justices Douglas and Goldberg, in concurring, contended that the "equal protection of the laws" clause of Amendment Fourteen and the latter's §5 (the "enforcement by appropriate legislation" power) also applied.

[164] For a table excerpting, comparing, and contrasting the Acts of 1957, 1960, and 1964, see John H. Ferguson and Dean E. McHenry, *The American System of Government*, 13th ed. (New York: McGraw-Hill Book Co., 1977), pp. 193–94.

[165] With the recently sworn-in Mr. Justice John Paul Stevens not participating, the Court addressed itself, albeit obviously somewhat uncomfortably, to the long-smoldering inherent seniority issue in a landmark decision in 1976. Speaking through Mr. Justice Brennan, the 5:3 majority (consisting also of Justices Stewart, White, Marshall, and Blackmun) ruled that blacks who were denied jobs in violation of Title VII (see p. 348, *supra*) of the 1964 statute, must be awarded *retroactive seniority* once they succeeded in obtaining those jobs. The majority held that blacks must thus be given the same seniority they would have had if they had been hired initially, with all accompanying rights, including pension benefits—even if this means that some whites, hired *after* the blacks' initial job applications, but *before* the blacks entered the jobs, would thereby now have less security and job protection. (*Franks v. Bowman Transportation Co.*, 434 U.S. 747.) Partly dissenting, together with Justices Powell and Rehnquist, Mr. Chief Justice Burger saw a clearcut case of reverse discrimination, commenting that "I cannot join in judicial approval of 'robbing Peter to pay Paul.'" (*Ibid.*, at 4366.) But *cf.* the 1977 *Teamster* rulings (*Teamsters v. United States* and *T.I.M.E.–D.C., Inc. v. United States*, 431 U.S. 324)! Their gist was that unless a seniority plan *intentionally* discriminates among workers it is *not* illegal under Title VII. The Court reconfirmed this posture 4:3 in 1980 in the instance of the California brewing industry system. (*California Brewers Association v. Bryant*, 444 U.S. 598.) Thus, "neutral" seniority systems may legally perpetuate favored employment for white males where, as in these cases, the seniority systems had been operative *before* the Civil Rights Act of 1964 took effect in 1965. Of course, seniority systems that *deliberately* discriminate are illegal, whether they date from pre- or post-1964 days.

and with public accommodations. For here the basic issues of individual rights and of societal obligations were patently joined. No other sections of the statute, not even its voting and educational segments, stirred so much controversy and debate or attracted so many negative votes. However, Title VI, too, was bitterly attacked and its application questioned even by such staunch Northern liberals as Senate Majority Leader Mike Mansfield.[166] Indeed, given the implications of the aforementioned "preferential treatment" and "reverse discrimination," it was destined to become the focus of major national controversy during the early 1970s and into the 1980s, centering on legal and constitutional implications of the governmental role against the backdrop of the twin constitutional guarantees of liberty and equality.[167] After all, *both* are guarantees that are seminal to our society—and they do not readily lend themselves to facile line-drawing.

Toward the Civil Rights Act of 1968. Still more legislation was to come, legislation replete with provisions that promised to cause lively debate in and out of Congress. While conceding that the fruits of the 1964 Act—and the Voting Rights Act of 1965 (see pp. 352 ff., below)—were already "impressively apparent," President Johnson sent Congress his third civil rights bill in three years in 1966, noting the obvious: that discriminatory practices "still exist in many American communities." In a tough attempt to further egalitarian goals, the Civil Rights Bill of 1966's most contentious provision would have outlawed discrimination on either racial or religious grounds in the "purchase, rental, lease, financing, use and occupancy" of *all housing.* Chiefly because of the so-called open housing provision, the bill, although it had passed the House in a watered-down version by a vote of 259:157, died on the floor of the Senate[168]—against a backdrop of black riots and demonstrations in cities throughout the land, now predominantly in the North, and the rise of resentment to the new "black power" slogan that began to characterize much of the civil rights activity of that year.

[166] See John Herber's article in *The New York Times,* September 29, 1966, p. 1L.
[167] E.g., see the critical book-length treatments by Nathan Glazer, *Affirmative Discrimination* (New York: Basic Books, 1976); George C. Roche, III, *The Balancing Act: Quota Hiring in Higher Education* (La Salle, Ill.: Open Court Publishing Company, Inc., 1974); and Thomas Sowell, *Affirmative Action Reconsidered: Was It Necessary in Academia?* (Washington, D.C.: American Enterprise Institute, 1975). For supportive works, see Boris I. Bittker, *The Case for Black Reparations* (New York: Random House, 1973); Ronald Dworkin, *Taking Rights Seriously* (Cambridge: Harvard University Press, 1977); and Robert M. O'Neill, *Discriminating Against Discrimination* (Bloomington: Indiana University Press, 1975). More or less "neutral" are works such as M. Cohen, T. Nagel, and T. Scanlon (eds.), *Equality and Preferential Treatment* (Princeton: Princeton University Press, 1977); Allan P. Sindler, *Bakke, De Funis, and Minority Admissions: The Quest for Equal Opportunity* (New York: Longman, Inc., 1978); and Ralph A. Rossum, *Reverse Discrimination: The Constitutional Debate* (New York: Marcel Dekker, Inc., 1980).
[168] Twice the Senate refused to shut off debate on the measure that September; the votes were 54:42 and 54:41—both short of the needed two-thirds.

Undaunted, President Johnson submitted a new bill in 1967, empha-
sizing the controversial housing issue. It failed to pass, but became law on
April 10, 1968–six days after the assassination of Dr. Martin Luther King,
Jr., and one day after his burial. Styled "a memorial to the fallen leader"
by the President, the 1968 Act significantly broadened existing federal
criminal laws dealing with civil rights, cataloguing a whole range of fed-
erally protected activities; articulated Indian rights; and addressed itself to
the rising tide of rioting and civil disobedience. But its most notable provision, certainly in terms of the yearnings of most blacks, was that on fair
housing which, with certain limited exemptions,[169] outlawed discrimination
in the *sale or rental* of *all housing*–not just in public or public-aided
housing–because of race, color, religion, or national origin. As if to confirm its legitimacy, even in advance of any litigation involving it on its
docket, the Supreme Court, just two months later, ruled 7:2 that, under
the almost-forgotten 102-year-old Civil Rights Act of 1866–enacted under
the enforcement provisions of the Thirteenth Amendment–racial discrimination in the purchase, lease, sale, holding, and conveyance of real and
personal property was expressly forbidden.[170] And in 1980 Congress moved
to toughen and speed the 1968 statute's available administrative enforcement powers.

The Quest for Suffrage

A good many sincere as well as fair-weather friends of black equality
prior to the decision to concentrate on education had insisted that it would
be wiser to direct the thrust of the movement toward suffrage, arguing that
effective suffrage would almost automatically rectify most, if not all, of the
black grievances in the public sector, the private sector ultimately following. This feeling that NAACP strategists and their supporters committed a
fundamental error persists in many circles to this day. Whatever the argument's merit, the suffrage problem was not really tackled until the Civil
Rights Acts of 1957, 1960, and 1964 had become law–and not effectively
until the passage of the Voting Rights Act of 1965.

ANTECEDENTS TO THE VOTING RIGHTS ACT OF 1965

Our nation's history is replete with systematic disfranchisement of blacks,
particularly in the South and the Border states. Although prior to the Civil

---

[169] See §§803 (b) and 807 of Title VIII of Public Law 90–284, 82 Stat. 73.

[170] *Jones v. Alfred H. Mayer Co.,* 392 U.S. 409 (1968). In a stinging dissenting
opinion, joined by Mr. Justice White, Mr. Justice Harlan flayed the majority for
proceeding "with such precipitous and insecure strides." He doubted that the 1866
law's "goals could constitutionally be achieved under the Thirteenth Amendment."
(At 476.) In that connection, see the Court's 1976 decisions in *Hills v. Gautreaux,*
p. 345, footnote 150, *supra* and, especially, in *Runyon v. McCrary,* pp. 388 ff., *infra.*

War, especially in the early decades following the adoption of the Constitution, other groups, too, had experienced considerable difficulty in their quest for suffrage—e.g., Quakers, Catholics, and Jews—blacks more than any other single minority group suffered second-class political citizenship. And, as we have seen, despite the enactment of the Civil War Amendments—in particular the Fifteenth, which specifically and expressly provided, as the Fourteenth had not,[171] that the "right of citizens of the United States to vote shall not be denied or abridged by the United States or by any State on account of race, color, or previous condition of servitude"—blacks continued to find access to the ballot box difficult, and often impossible, in much of the old Confederacy. That access had been all but closed by the turn of the century, if not directly then indirectly by resort to assorted devices such as the "grandfather clause," the "white primary," the poll tax, interpretation clauses, understanding clauses, and sundry other registration requirements—a seemingly inexhaustible array of covert as well as overt tools of discrimination.[172]

Until the legislative activity in the 1950s, much of this discrimination was rendered feasible by our federal structure. An important distinction existed between the legal right to vote for *federal* officials and the legal right to vote for *local* and *state* officials. The latter vote stems from state constitutions and laws and is thus not on its face a federal right in the same sense and to the same degree as the right to vote for federal officers, such as members of Congress and Presidential electors. Hence, at least until enactment of the four recent Civil Rights Acts and, more pertinently, the Voting Rights Act of 1965 and its subsequent strengthening amendments of 1970 and 1975 the states were free to define their own qualifications for voting for state and local officials, and in part also for their federal representatives. This state power was subject only to the limitations of Amendments Fourteen, Fifteen, Nineteen, and Twenty-Four and that intriguing Article One, Section 4. The latter, while granting the "Times, Places, and Manner" of holding elections for federal officials to the states, also contains a clause that would become an important tool in the judicial arsenal of aid to blacks: "but the Congress may at any time by Law make or alter such Regulations, except as to the Places of chusing Senators."

When access to the ballot remained foreclosed to blacks because they continued to be denied their rightful influence in Southern politics, and when Congress failed to come to their aid, they turned to the federal *courts* for redress. Initially they found little because of a then unsympa-

---

[171] See the discussion in Berger, *op. cit.,* Chapters 4 and 5.

[172] For data on black registration and the denial of voting rights to blacks, see, among others, the 1959 *Report* and the 1961 voting study of the United States Commission on Civil Rights; subsequent annual *Reports;* and those by the U.S. Bureau of the Census.

thetic judiciary and of an absence of appropriate precedent. When the Supreme Court rejected a promising challenge to the Mississippi literacy test in 1898,[173] matters looked bleak indeed. As recently as 1959, the literacy device was upheld unanimously by the Court in a North Carolina case,[174] in an opinion written by no less firm an exponent of black equality than Mr. Justice Douglas!

Light Ahead. Moving toward the 1950s and 1960s when blacks were to win equal rights at least on paper and at the bar of the judiciary in all parts of the land, an important judicial tool proved to be the Fifteenth Amendment—although the crucial one, as in the education struggles, became the "equal protection of the laws" clause of Amendment Fourteen, notwithstanding its legislative history of excluding black suffrage from its intended reach.[175] Still, in 1915 the Supreme Court had based its decision on the clearcut language of the Fifteenth Amendment when in a unanimous opinion by Mr. Chief Justice Edward D. White it struck down the Oklahoma "grandfather clause."[176] This transparent device, adopted in several Southern and Border states, provided a convenient loophole through which illiterate whites could escape the provisions of literacy tests. It exempted from those tests all "persons and their lineal descendants" who were qualified to vote as of January 1, 1866, or any similarly convenient date prior to Amendments Fourteen and Fifteen, which would not apply to blacks. The words "Negro," "black," or "colored" did not appear anywhere in the various grandfather clauses, because practically no blacks, if any, voted or were able to vote before the Civil War.

After the failure of an attempt to resuscitate its spirit, if not its letter, in 1939,[177] the grandfather clause was indeed gone. But the poll tax, the "white primary," and a number of other devices remained available to those state officers bent upon the perpetuation of a pure or almost-pure white suffrage. A windfall came their way in 1921 when a narrowly divided Supreme Court ruled—in a messy Michigan Senatorial primary case, involving Henry Ford and Truman H. Newberry[178]—that Congress had no power, or at best highly dubious power, to regulate *primary* elections in the states, be they for federal or state or local office. Although the litigation itself dealt with fraud rather than racial discrimination, the decision was tailor-made for the devotees of the white primary. Hence Texas went to work at once and passed the blatant Texas White Primary Law of 1924, which read: "In no event shall a negro be eligible to participate in a Democratic primary election in the State of Texas, and should a negro vote in

---

173 *Williams v. Mississippi,* 170 U.S. 213 (1898).
174 *Lassiter v. Northampton Election Board,* 360 U.S. 45.
175 See Berger, *op. cit.,* data in Chapters 4 and 5.
176 *Guinn v. United States,* 238 U.S. 347.
177 *Lane v. Wilson,* 307 U.S. 268.
178 *Newberry v. United States,* 256 U.S. 232.

a Democratic primary election, such ballot shall be void and election officials shall not count the same."

A black physician from El Paso, Dr. L. A. Nixon, took up the fight.
Denied participation in the Democratic Party's primary under the terms of
the Texas law, Dr. Nixon challenged its constitutionality. In a 9:0 opinion,
written by Mr. Justice Holmes in 1927, the Supreme Court agreed. Without passing on the matter of primaries *versus* general elections, so importantly present in the Michigan decision,[179] the Court declared the Texas
White Primary Law unconstitutional as a "direct and obvious infringe-
ment" of the "equal protection of the laws" clause of the Fourteenth
Amendment. Here, then, that important clause entered the fray in the
voting field—fully a decade prior to its first meaningful utilization in the
area of educational segregation.[180]

Texas was not so easily discouraged, however: it repealed the 1924
statute and substituted a measure authorizing the State Executive Committee of every political party to "prescribe the qualifications of its own members." The state's Democratic Party then promptly "prescribed" that "only
whites" shall be eligible in *its* primaries. When Dr. Nixon thus again was
denied participation in the party of his choice, he returned to court with a
constitutional challenge to Texas's enabling statute. The Supreme Court,
speaking through Mr. Justice Cardozo, soon struck down this latest Texas
device (albeit this time by the narrowest of margins, 5:4) on the grounds
that by setting qualifications the Democratic Party was usurping state law
and that, consequently, the State of Texas had in fact *acted through* the
Party as its agent, thereby violating once again the "equal protection of
the laws" clause of the Fourteenth Amendment.[181] Not to be outdone,
Texas then (1932) *repealed* the authorizing clause of the above legislation. Its Democratic Party, in turn, acting through the *Democratic State
Convention,* on its own authority and without any statutory sanction,
adopted a resolution to render itself a "private group," permitting as members of this *private group* only *white* persons. When this arrangement also
was challenged at the bar of our highest tribunal, the Court unanimously
accepted the constitutionality of this new loophole on the grounds that the
State of Texas was not involved: that the private group referred to was not
a "creature of the state" but a *voluntary association* that had acted on its
own. This appeared to settle the matter at issue, for, as Mr. Justice Roberts
wrote for the Court, "private persons or groups cannot violate the Fourteenth Amendment," in the absence of state action *per se.*[182]

But this seeming triumph of the disfranchisers was short-lived. In 1941,

[179] *Newberry v. United States, ibid.*
[180] *Nixon v. Herndon,* 273 U.S. 536.
[181] *Nixon v. Condon,* 286 U.S. 73 (1932).
[182] *Grovey v. Townsend,* 295 U.S. 45 (1935), at 52.

just six years after the *"Private Group"* decision, the Supreme Court was confronted with a case of fraud in a Louisiana *federal* primary. A Louisiana election official, one Patrick B. Classic, had crudely transferred ninety-seven votes cast validly for two candidates in that primary to a third candidate—his own choice! In its 5:3 holding the Court, through Mr. Justice Stone, ruled that the above-mentioned Section 4 of the Constitution's Article One in fact authorized Congress to regulate *primaries* as well as *elections* because "primaries" in the words of the Constitution were tantamount to "elections" and, being "an integral part of the election machinery," were subject to congressional regulations.[183] This decision did not, to be sure, settle the question whether whites were legally at liberty to exclude blacks from primaries for state and local officials, for the race question was not involved. What the *Classic* decision did do—and it was a truly significant accomplishment in constitutional interpretation—was to pave the way for federal regulation by overruling the *Newberry* (Michigan) holding, which had separated the concept of federal "primaries" from "elections."[184] The *Grovey v. Townsend "Private Group"* case[185] still stood, however.

The White Primary Falls. Yet three years later, in the case of *Smith v. Allwright*,[186] the Supreme Court in an 8:1 opinion written by Mr. Justice Reed—a Border state Democrat from Kentucky[187]—declared the Texas white primary unconstitutional as a violation of the *Fifteenth Amendment.* Smith, a black, had been denied participation by a Texas election judge, Allwright, who relied on the "voluntary association" concept developed by the Court in the *Grovey* decision. But now that Court ruled that, in effect, the Democratic Party of the State of Texas was acting as an *agent of the state* because of the character of its duties—such as providing election machinery—and was thus subject to the pertinent provisions of Amendments Fourteen and Fifteen, here the latter. In the *Classic* case,[188] the Court had set up two alternate or complementary "tests" to determine whether or not a primary was validly affected, and thus regulatable, by the provisions of federal authority under the Constitution: (A) had the state law made the primary an integral part of the election machinery; and/or (B) did the primary "effectively control the choice."[189] Now in *Allwright both* tests ap-

183 *United States v. Classic,* 313 U.S. 299 (1941), at 318.

184 *Newberry v. United States,* 256 U.S. 232 (1921).

185 *Grovey v. Townsend, op. cit.*

186 321 U.S. 649 (1944).

187 For a fascinating account, demonstrating that the case had originally been assigned to Mr. Justice Frankfurter but then re-assigned for "strategic" reasons to Mr. Justice Reed, see Alpheus T. Mason, *Harlan Fiske Stone: Pillar of the Law* (New York: Viking Press, 1956), p. 615. (It is also related in my *The Judicial Process, op. cit.,* pp. 221–22.)

188 *United States v. Classic, op. cit.*

189 *Ibid.,* at 318.

plied! The Court admonished Texas and the nation that the constitutional right to be free from racial discrimination in voting

> is not to be nullified by a state through casting its electoral process in a form which permits a private organization to practice racial discrimination in the election. . . . It may be taken as a postulate that the right to vote in . . . a primary . . . without discrimination by the State . . . is a right secured by the Constitution.[190]

As had been true of the *Grovey "Private Group"* case,[191] the controlling issue had to be the answer to the basic question: had the black claimant involved thereby been barred from the primary by *state* action? The Supreme Court held that he had—and *Grovey* was thus overruled, nine years after it had become law. Only Mr. Justice Roberts dissented from the *Allwright* decision—and he did so as much on grounds of judicial "self-restraint" as on the merits of the controversy, grumbling that "Supreme Court decisions are becoming in the same class as a restricted railroad ticket, good for this day and train only."[192]

The *Smith v. Allwright* decision did much to stimulate black participation in primary elections in the South and the Border states; but the forces of exclusion were far from ineffective, and ingenuity was not lacking. For example, in an attempt to perpetuate white hegemony at the polls and, concurrently, to test the *Allwright* ruling further, South Carolina promptly *repealed* all of its 147 laws and one constitutional provision relating to the conduct of primaries. But a courageous United States District Court jurist, J. Waties Waring—a tenth-generation member of the South Carolina aristocracy—held in 1947 in *Rice v. Elmore*[193] that the South Carolina primaries, though denuded of state authorization *per se,* "effectively control the choice" of candidates for public office. This finding satisfied Test B of *Classic* case,[194] and Waring ruled, consequently, that the denial to blacks of their right to vote in primaries was *prima facie* evidence of a violation of both the Fourteenth and Fifteenth Amendments. On appeal, the United States Court of Appeals for the Fourth Circuit sitting in Richmond, Virginia, sustained Judge Waring.[195] That opinion was written by Chief Judge John J. Parker—ironically the same man who had been rejected as President Hoover's nominee to the United States Supreme Court in 1930, by a 41:39 vote, in part because of his alleged anti-black bias.[196] And the Su-

---

[190] *Smith v. Allwright,* 321 U.S. 649 (1944), at 661, 664.
[191] *Grovey v. Townsend, op. cit.*
[192] *Smith v. Allwright, op. cit.,* at 669.
[193] 72 F. Supp. 516 (1947).
[194] *United States v. Classic, op. cit.*
[195] *Rice v. Elmore,* 165 F. 2d 387 (1947).
[196] See my *The Judicial Process, op. cit.,* pp. 84–88. The next rejectees were President Nixon's 1969 and 1970 nominations of Clement H. Haynsworth and G. Harrold

preme Court refused to review the *Elmore* case,[197] thus letting Waring's holding stand. As a result 35,000 blacks came to the polls in South Carolina's Democratic primary in 1948. Judge Waring, now harassed, pilloried, and isolated, found it necessary five years later to leave his old home and his beloved bench to move with his family to New York. "My ostracism was total," he recalled wistfully in a 1963 interview. "After my racial cases it got very lonely."[198]

Yet, undeterred by the decision in *Rice v. Elmore,* South Carolina sought to evade it by vesting control of primaries in private clubs to which blacks were not admitted. As a prerequisite to voting in primaries, these clubs required the taking of an oath that was particularly odious to blacks. Among other things, it was necessary to swear to a belief in the social and educational separation of the races. Predictably, this effort to continue disfranchisement of non-whites also ran afoul of effective judicial vetoes in 1948 and 1949.[199] And in 1953 a much more elaborate and less obvious device used to keep blacks from voting in Ford Bend County, Texas, fell: the "pre-primary primary," conducted by a group known as the "Jaybird Democratic Association."[200] Few could continue to doubt that the federal authorities really meant business in the voting field. Still, the various shenanigans continued, often taking the form of "understanding" and "interpreting" clauses, which were destined to fall, too, sooner or later.[201] Then, of course, there was the poll tax—a device more difficult to indict; it had been specifically *upheld* by the Supreme Court both in 1937[202] and in 1951.[203] While it was perhaps the best known of the several devices, it was the least important. When it was outlawed for *federal* elections by the Twenty-Fourth or Holland Amendment,[204] ratified in January 1964, its Southern presence was confined to Alabama, Arkansas, Mississippi, Texas, and Virginia. But even for *state* elections its days were numbered: when the question of the constitutionality of the Virginia state poll tax, as applied to state elections, reached the Supreme Court in 1966, the tax was

---

Carswell, by votes of 55:45 and 51:45, respectively. See my *Justices and Presidents: A Political History of Appointments to the Supreme Court* (New York: Oxford University Press, 1974, and Penguin, 1975).

[197] *Rice v. Elmore,* 333 U.S. 875 (1948), *certiorari* denied.

[198] *The Greenwich* (Conn.) *Times,* Aug. 30, 1963, p. 13—interviewed by Charles L. West. When he died in 1968, his Charleston, South Carolina, burial was attended by 200 blacks and fewer than a dozen whites.

[199] *Brown v. Baskin,* 78 F. Supp. 933 (1948) and 174 F. 2d 391 (1949).

[200] *Terry v. Adams,* 345 U.S. 461 (1953). For an explanatory article, see Luther A. Huston, "High Court Upsets a Limited Primary," *The New York Times,* May 5, 1953, p. 19*l.*

[201] E.g., *Schnell v. Davis,* 336 U.S. 933 (1949).

[202] *Breedlove v. Suttles,* 302 U.S. 277, involving a *white* male Georgian.

[203] *Butler v. Thompson,* 341 U.S. 937.

[204] Named after U.S. Senator Spessard Holland (D.-Fla.), who "fathered" it.

given a prompt judicial burial.[205] Appropriately, it was Mr. Justice Douglas, the sole dissenter when the Court had upheld the Virginia tax fifteen years before,[206] who spoke for the six-man majority. Avoiding the First Amendment issue urged upon the Court by the then Solicitor-General Thurgood Marshall, Douglas leaned heavily on the Court's newly developed "one man, one vote" doctrine[207] for his authority that Virginia's $1.50 tax as a prerequisite for voting in state elections violated the "equal protection of the laws" guarantee of the Fourteenth Amendment. Interestingly, although the plaintiffs in the two cases before the Court were black, the majority's holding was based on *economic* rather than on racial discrimination. "To introduce wealth or payment of a fee as a measure of a voter's qualifications," wrote Douglas, "is to introduce a capricious or irrelevant factor. The degree of the discrimination is irrelevant."[208] Justices Black, Harlan, and Stewart, on the other hand, while dissenting on varying grounds, all agreed that "non-discriminatory and fairly applied" payment of a poll tax *could* be a reasonable basis for determining the right to vote.[209]

The problem with the literacy test—in itself neither unreasonable nor discriminatory (something that could be said, at least in theory, of several of the devices used to disfranchise)—was its *application;* it was frequently used for gross discrimination against blacks. Its "non-discriminatory" principle was upheld by the United States Supreme Court as late as 1959,[210] and, as we shall see, when the Voting Rights Act of 1965 launched a selective assault upon the literacy test, almost one-half of the states of the Union were using a variety of such tests. Although it is perhaps easier to attack the concept of the literacy test as a necessary and desirable suffrage requirement than it is to attack the more essential requirements of residence[211] and registration, it would be unfair to condemn it on its face. There are other causes for non-voting than racial discrimination; apathy, for example, is the chief cause of low participation by the American electorate—averaging barely 50 per cent of those eligible to vote even in presi-

---

[205] *Harper v. Virginia State Board of Elections,* 383 U.S. 663 (decided March 25, 1966).

[206] *Butler v. Thompson, op. cit.*

[207] *Gray v. Sanders,* 372 U.S. 368 (1963), at 381. See pp. 19–20, *supra.* (Mr. Justice Stewart preferred the term "one voter, one vote"; Mr. Chief Justice Warren often used "one man, one vote," the most commonly employed terminology; Mr. Justice Douglas alternated between the nouns "person" and "man.")

[208] *Harper v. Virginia Board of Elections, op. cit.,* at 668.

[209] See the separate dissenting opinions by Justices Black and Harlan, *ibid.,* at 670 and 680. The former objected to what he viewed as the majority's "natural law" approach vis-à-vis "reasonableness"; the latter believed a constitutional amendment to be necessary.

[210] *Lassiter v. Northampton Election Board,* 360 U.S. 45 (a North Carolina case).

[211] Affirmed by the Court in a Maryland (one-year) test case in 1965 (*Deueding v. Devlin,* 380 U.S. 125). But see the 1970 federal statute, pp. 364–65, *infra.*

dential elections. However, the privilege of voting also contains the privilege of abstinence, of course.[212]

The Voting Rights Act of 1965. Regardless of the weight one might assign to any one of the various factors that caused the demonstrably low black suffrage, mid-20th-century statistics serve well as an indictment of a state of affairs that cried out for government action above and beyond the four Civil Rights Acts of 1957, 1960, 1964, and 1968. The presidential election year of 1948 saw barely 600,000 blacks registered in the eleven states of the South, a mere 12 per cent of those of voting age; 1952 saw close to 1,000,000, some 20 per cent; and 1956 roughly 1,250,000, or 25 per cent. Sixty per cent of the eligible whites were registered in the same region. Although the percentage of blacks *registered* continued to climb— reaching 27 per cent by 1961 and 40 per cent just prior to the enactment of the Voting Rights Act of 1965—the die-hard resistance to *any* registration in widespread and important areas of the South, particularly in most of Mississippi, much of Alabama, and a good many counties of Louisiana, continued to rankle civil rights leaders. As late as the summer of 1965, a mere 6.8 per cent of eligible blacks had been registered in Mississippi, an increase of scarcely 2 per cent after more than four years of activity and three federal statutes.[213]

Counsels of patience were now clearly falling on deaf ears; the civil rights movement had begun to take to the streets in 1960; and then, in early 1965, the town of Selma, Alabama, became the catalyst for the new voting law. Civil rights leaders, headed by Dr. Martin Luther King, organized a well-advertised 50-mile march from Selma to Montgomery in support of efforts to obtain greater black voter registration in the face of continued difficulty, defiance, and procrastination. The march began on March 7, only to be brutally broken up by Alabama state troopers, under orders of Governor George C. Wallace, while it was still close to Selma. Employing whips, night sticks, cattle-prods, and tear gas, the troopers injured at least forty of the marchers. The scene flashed on the television screens of homes throughout the nation and the world. Widespread revulsion set in at once and hundreds of additional civil rights supporters, many of them white clergy of all faiths, poured into the Selma area. Tragedy was not long in coming: a white Unitarian minister from Boston, the Reverend James J. Reeb, was fatally clubbed down on a Selma street by irate white

[212] For a discussion of the problem of participation, including the issue of compulsory voting, see my *Compulsory Voting* (Washington, D.C.: Public Affairs Press, 1955).

[213] Statistics are obtainable from numerous sources, among them the Southern Regional Council, the *Race Relations Reporter,* various almanacs, the daily press, the *Statistical Abstract of the United States,* and annual compendia by the United States Commission on Civil Rights, the American Civil Liberties Union, the American Jewish Congress, and numerous other groups.

natives. Civil rights leaders then rescheduled the march, and President Johnson ordered the Alabama National Guard into federal service to protect the marchers. Again led by Dr. King, the march was completed peacefully on the 25th, with a crowd of 30,000 gathering on the steps of the Alabama capitol in Montgomery. But on the same night a white woman from Detroit, Mrs. Viola Liuzzo, who was shuttling blacks back to Selma from Montgomery in her car, was shot and killed by a trio of white ambushers.

Ten days later, responding to public clamor for action following the Selma outrages,[214] President Johnson addressed Congress in an extraordinary Joint Session, calling for the enactment of the strongest voting rights legislation proposed in nine decades. "The time for waiting is gone," the President told his hushed audience, "outside this chamber is the outraged conscience of a nation—the grave concern of many nations—and the harsh judgment of history on our acts."[215] Against this background his administration submitted the Voting Rights Bill of 1965, based on the Fifteenth Amendment's exhortation that no person shall be denied the right to vote because of "race, color, or previous condition of servitude," and giving Congress the power to enforce its provisions "by appropriate legislation."

The bill became law in August, and it was a tough one. It had passed the Senate by a vote of 79:18 and the House of Representatives by 328:74 —an even more decisive margin than in the enactment of the Civil Rights Act of 1964—and contained these key provisions:

> It barred literacy and other tests for voting deemed to be discriminatory, based on a rather complicated formula that affected six states in the deep South: Alabama, Georgia, Mississippi, Louisiana, South Carolina, and Virginia; thirty-four counties in North Carolina; all of Alaska; and single counties in Maine, Arizona, and Idaho. (The formula concerning literacy tests extended only to those areas where such tests were in force November 1, 1964, *and* where less than 50 per cent of the voting age population voted, or were registered to vote, in the 1964 presidential election.)

> It set up new criminal penalties for attempts to keep qualified persons from voting or to threaten or harm civil rights workers assisting potential voters.

> It directed the U.S. Department of Justice to begin court suits challenging the constitutionality of poll taxes still used in *state and local* elections. (Arkansas having by then abandoned the poll tax, this provision was directed at Alabama, Mississippi, Texas, and Virginia.)

[214] It is poetic justice that the 1972 elections—just seven years after Selma—would show that the greatest political gains for Southern blacks had come in Alabama, generally, and in Selma, in particular: that year 117 blacks were elected to Alabama offices, and in Selma—where the black registration had risen from 2.3 per cent in 1965 to 67 per cent (!) in 1972—five of the ten city council seats were won by blacks. In 1976 over 200 blacks held elective office in Alabama; double that number in 1980.

[215] As quoted in *The New York Times,* March 16, 1965, p. 1*l*.

Clearly, the fundamental purpose of the Voting Rights Act of 1965, the passage of which President Johnson termed a "proud moment for this nation," was to facilitate black registration and voting by the elimination, in those states where discrimination had been proved to be both most rampant and most persistent, of all requirements but the basic ones of age, residence, mental competence, and absence of a criminal record. Needless to say, this and some other provisions[216] of the Act raised serious problems of constitutionality—given the somewhat murky division of responsibility for suffrage between the federal and state governments. South Carolina quickly brought suit, though it seemed hardly likely that the Supreme Court would strike down legislation that, however marginal in constitutional interpretation in some of its aspects, was still clearly based upon the letter and spirit of the Fifteenth Amendment—adopted some ninety-five years before. The Court's answer came rapidly and, as anticipated, approvingly: with Mr. Justice Black dissenting in part (on the law's appeals procedure) and concurring in part, the Court upheld the seven major provisions of the Act in a 31-page opinion written by Mr. Chief Justice Warren.[217] He based his ruling squarely on the Act's constitutionality and, predictably, on the power of Congress to act under the provisions of the Fifteenth Amendment. The Chief Justice wrote that two points "emerge vividly" from the voluminous legislative history of the Act: (1) that Congress felt itself "confronted by an insidious and pervasive evil which had been perpetuated in certain parts of our country by unremitting and ingenious defiance of the Constitution"; and (2) that Congress demonstrably concluded that the unsuccessful remedies which it had prescribed in the past would have to be replaced by "sterner and more elaborate measures."[218] "We may finally look forward to the day," summarized the Chief Justice, quoting verbatim the commands of Amendment Fifteen, "when

[216] One of the most contentious was the Kennedy (Robert F.) amendment to the statute, which specifically granted the right to vote to Puerto Ricans, of whom 750,000 then lived in New York City, provided they had a sixth-grade education from a Puerto Rican school—in which Spanish is the principal language, of course. In effect, the amendment circumvented the then otherwise legal New York literacy test. A three-judge federal district court, one judge dissenting, declared that section of the Voting Rights Act unconstitutional in November 1965 (247 F. Supp. 196). However, in a 7:2 opinion, written by Mr. Justice Brennan with Justices Harlan and Stewart dissenting (they believed that *the Court* rather than Congress should have determined the constitutionality of the New York literacy law), the Supreme Court reversed the lower tribunal, concluding that Congress in passing the special Spanish literacy amendment to the bill had acted legally because it was "appropriate legislation . . . plainly adapted" to the enforcement of the equal protection of the laws clause of the Fourteenth Amendment and otherwise consistent with the letter and spirit of the "positive grant of legislative power" to Congress inherent in that amendment to the Constitution. (*Katzenbach v. Morgan*, 384 U.S. 641, 1966.)

[217] *South Carolina v. Katzenbach*, 383 U.S. 301 (1966).

[218] *Ibid.*, at 309.

truly the right of citizens of the United States to vote shall not be denied or abridged by the United States or by any state on account of race, color, or previous condition of servitude."[219]

The Voting Rights Act of 1965 had hardly become law when the Johnson Administration commenced its enforcement with two steps. First, literacy tests were suspended as a prerequisite to voting in seven states (Alabama, Alaska,[220] Georgia, Louisiana, Mississippi, South Carolina, and Virginia), twenty-six counties of North Carolina, and one in Arizona; second, the Department of Justice, true to its mandate under the Act, filed suits to abolish the poll tax in the four states that still had one: Alabama, Mississippi, Texas, and Virginia. Moreover, under the provisions of the law, some forty-five *federal voting examiners,* all employees of the United States Civil Service Commission, were standing by in the deep South, waiting to move into fifteen to twenty counties that had a history of resistance to black voting. The examiners, working in teams, began to register eligible blacks that August within a matter of days. Results were almost immediately apparent: on the first supervised registration day under the new statute, 1,144 blacks were enrolled in nine counties with a history of rampant discrimination in Alabama, Louisiana, and Mississippi—an increase of 65 per cent! Extending their work to four other counties, the federal voting examiners had registered almost 20,000 blacks within ten days. In the first two months after the enactment of the new voting law, about 110,000 blacks were registered voluntarily by *local officials* and more than 56,000 by the federal examiners sent to areas designed by Attorney-General Nicholas Katzenbach. It was in the May 1966 primaries that, for the first time, blacks voted in large numbers in the deep South—and in six Southern states they elected some of their candidates to office.

By March 1966, under pressure of the new law, federal examiners had enrolled 101,370 blacks; local registrars another 201,000. That November, the percentage of eligible blacks registered to vote in the South ranged from 27.8 per cent in Mississippi and 48.9 in Alabama to 71.7 per cent in Tennessee, averaging 50.1 per cent. Although the apathy and fear by blacks about voting, which had been so firmly established by decades of white exclusionary rule, could not be eradicated overnight, Southern black

---

[219] *Ibid.,* at 337.

[220] On May 24, 1966, Alaska became the first state to be exempted from the Act's literacy test suspension provisions when it convinced the Department of Justice that its literacy test had never been used to deny the right to vote on the basis of race or color. Virginia requested repeatedly to be exempted. Unsuccessful, it ultimately went to the Supreme Court (*Virginia v. United States,* 420 U.S. 901) which, however, without hearing oral argument, in 1975 affirmed 6:3 a lower federal court's decision denying Virginia's plea. (Dissenting were Mr. Chief Justice Burger and Justices Powell and Rehnquist.)

registration had now reached 2,671,514, fully 1,200,000 more than as of July 1960.[221]

The 1970 Amendments. The success of the 1965 statute heralded a fierce legislative battle to extend and amend it upon its termination five years later. Predictably, pro and con forces jockeyed for broadening and for gutting it, respectively. The resultant legislation was a compromise; but, by and large, the line was drawn in favor of the aspirations of the still unfranchised or under-franchised. Continued for five years, the amended statute, in its main provisions:

> extended the franchise in both federal *and* state elections to 18-year-olds;[222]

> extended the 1965 prohibition against the use of literacy tests as a condition to voting registration to *all* fifty states until 1975 (thus removing the "selective stigma" of the 1965 provision);[223]

> established a thirty-day limit for *residency* requirements in *Presidential* elections.[224]

By fall 1971, the new voting laws had added 1.5 million blacks and 6 of the 11 million 18- to 21-year-old voters. By Presidential election time 1972 the figures for Southern blacks had risen to 3,448,565,[225] reaching well above 3.5 million for the November 1974 "off-year" races.[226] The total of *all* blacks registered reached 8 million less than a year later.[227]

The 1975 Amendments. When the so demonstrably successful statute came up for renewal in 1975, the question was not whether it would be extended but to what degree it would be broadened even more. By thumping majorities Congress did both in mid-1975. Exactly ten years after

---

[221] *The New York Times,* July 27, 1966, p. 25*l*, and November 27, 1966, p. 74*l*. By September 1, 1966, a total of 1,147,236 blacks had registered in the five "black belt" states of Mississippi, Alabama, Georgia, Louisiana, and South Carolina, compared with 687,000 when the Voting Rights Act of 1965 became law one year earlier. (*Ibid.,* October 21, 1966, p. 1*l*.) An additional 210,000 had been added to the rolls three years later. (*Ibid.,* December 14, 1969, p. 1*l*.)

[222] Late in December 1970 the Supreme Court upheld (5:4) the provision's *federal* applicability, but struck down (5:4) the *state* aspect. (*Oregon v. Mitchell,* 400 U.S. 112), Mr. Justice Black providing the swing vote in both instances.

[223] Upheld by the Court (8:1) in *United States v. Arizona,* 400 U.S. 112 (1970).

[224] Upheld by the Court (9:0) in *United States v. Idaho,* 400 U.S. 112 (1970). In 1972 it extended this interpretation (6:1) to reach *state* and local elections (*Dunn v. Blumstein,* 405 U.S. 330.) On the other hand, it upheld (6:3) the fifty-day pre-election registration requirements for state and local elections in Arizona and Georgia. (*Marston v. Lewis* and *Burns v. Fortson,* 410 U.S. 679.) It also upheld (5:4) a New York State requirement of a *pre-primary* registration period of eight to eleven months. (October 22, 1974.)

[225] Charles V. Hamilton, *The Bench and the Ballot: Southern Federal Judges and Black Voters* (New York: Oxford University Press, 1973), p. vii.

[226] *The New York Times,* November 11, 1974, p. 30c.

[227] U.S. Bureau of the Census, *Annual Report,* 1975.

President Johnson signed the original Voting Rights Act, President Ford affixed his signature to a new extension, this time for seven rather than five years, that substantially broadened the law by:

permanently prohibiting literacy tests anywhere;

bringing Spanish, Filipino, Chinese, Japanese, and Korean-Americans, American Indians, Alaskan natives, and other minorities under its coverage;

bracketing additional states, or parts thereof—a total of 35—under its pre-clearance provisions[228] in the case of any state-sponsored attempts to change existing voting laws (added were heretofore not included parts of *thirty* states, ranging from Arizona through Wyoming);

allowing private citizens to file suit to bring their local jurisdictions under the law's protection;

mandating bilingual ballots and election materials (or oral assistance in their absence) to the above-listed minority groups;[229]

empowering the Justice Department to intervene in jurisdictions covered by the Act when changes in voting procedures will result in minority-voter dilution.

By the beginning of the new decade, almost 10 million blacks were now on the voting rolls, coming within 9 per cent of the national figure of 70 per cent for whites, and within 7 per cent of the white voting turnout.[230]

NEW TACTICS FOR OLD PROBLEMS AND NEW ONES

The evolving desegregation process, described in the preceding pages, underwent a major change following that Opinion Monday on May 17, 1954, when Mr. Chief Justice Warren announced the Court's decision in *Brown v. Board of Education.*[231] The change in tactics began with the Montgomery bus boycott in December 1955, yet perhaps it became most dramatically evident with the Greensboro "sit-ins" early in 1960. Whatever its genesis, the protest movement was now clearly tired of delays, frustrated by creeping gradualism, angered by physical outrages. Militancy came to the forefront.

[228] Not applicable, however, if changes are formulated by the *courts*. (See, for example, the 1977 Mississippi reapportionment case of *Connor v. Finch,* 431 U.S. 407.)

[229] By 1975 the government had already ordered 529 counties and towns in twenty-six states to comply with that provision; and in 1976 the Justice Department ruled that 513 political jurisdictions in thirty states were affected. (*The New York Times,* April 22, 1976, p. 25c.)

[230] See the quarterly and annual reports, *Current Population Reports* and *Population Characteristics,* published by the Bureau of the Census of the U.S. Department of Commerce. Moves to extend the law to 1992 began in 1981.

[231] 347 U.S. 483.

Thus, the initiative for change shifted from a relatively few professional desegregationists, in such traditional organizations as the NAACP and the Urban League, to large numbers of average citizens who concluded that they had no choice but to do battle against "The System" by direct action "in the streets." This development both stemmed from and gave rise to a coterie of new, formally organized protest groups,[232] particularly the Southern Christian Leadership Conference (SCLC), which had been created in 1956–57 under the leadership of Dr. Martin Luther King, Jr.[233]

. The "sit-in" movement of 1960 had first illustrated the belief that only *action* would obtain results, a belief that became a firm conviction of these groups and their followers—action as a supplement or complement to the educational and legal means heretofore predominantly employed. Although the educational, and especially the legal, tools had produced significant results since World War II, they were nevertheless for Dr. King, other protest movement leaders, and their vast number of followers, too slow in producing change. Turning then to "action," the black leadership rapidly discovered that the development of community "crisis situations," such as economic boycotts by black protest movements, was usually at least partly successful simply because the crises demanded a speedy resolution by community decision makers. Yet "activism" was certain to raise serious problems in and for society—problems of the limits of civil disobedience—problems, once again, of where to draw the line.

Illustrations of New Tactics. Of course, some "action" had accompanied the movement for quite a while: there were sporadic rallies, marches, boycotts, and picket lines; but almost none really attained major significance.

Yet the Montgomery, Alabama, bus boycott, eighteen months after

---

[232] See the illuminating article by James H. Laue, "The Changing Character of Negro Protest," in 357 *The Annals of the American Academy of Political and Social Science* 119 (January 1965).

[233] Others were the Congress of Racial Equality (CORE), established in 1943; the Student Non-violent Coordinating Committee (SNCC), an "action" group founded in 1960; and the National Welfare Rights Organization (NWRO), established in 1968 (but dissolved after its founder, George Wiley, drowned in a boating accident in 1973). While SCLC under Dr. King's guidance steadfastly maintained its dedication to non-violence, CORE and especially SNCC proved to be not averse to violent action, as demonstrated from 1965 on under the direction of such fiery young leaders as CORE's Floyd McKissick and SNCC's Stokely Carmichael and H. Rap Brown. But after having been the pace-setter in the civil rights movement for eight years, SNCC, with a rural Southern origin, was largely displaced as of 1968 by the slum-born Black Panthers, a militant "black liberation" group: violence-prone, and small but potent. Additional groups were organized, with varying degrees of success, throughout the 1970s, some featuring the rise of highly visible, influential leaders, such as the Rev. Jesse Jackson, head of the Chicago-based PUSH. More than a thousand delegates from 34 states formed a new organization, the National Black United Front in mid-1980, "to pull together the diverse elements within black America, most of which have not succeeded." (*The New York Times,* June 30, 1980, p. B-13.)

Brown I, did. It was a stubborn, year-long boycott of the city's buses in protest against Montgomery's continued segregated seating practices. The action began when a black seamstress, Mrs. Rosa Parks—who was to become a symbol of the civil rights movement—refused to give up her seat to a white rider and was fined $10. Led by Dr. King, Montgomery's entire black community participated in the boycott. No longer willing to sit in the "Jim Crow" section, something they had done all their lives, they were ready to walk miles or wait hours for car pools. As one 72-year-old weary black woman said with ungrammatical profundity: "My feets is tired but my soul is at rest."[234] The boycott did not end until, one entire year later, segregation was outlawed by a federal court injunction, followed quickly by a Supreme Court decision that struck down as a violation of equal protection of the laws the Montgomery statute that had required segregation on motor buses operated within the city.[235] It is not astonishing that the successful Montgomery boycott set a precedent for similar actions in cities throughout the South, extending to retail stores, produce markets, and a host of other sales and service facilities.

Yet a boycott destined to be far more militant and far more controversial began on February 1, 1960, when four black freshmen[236] at North Carolina Agricultural and Technical College began what at first was a spontaneous "sit-in" demonstration at the lunch counter of F. W. Woolworth's dime store in Greensboro. They had asked for cups of coffee, and had done so politely, but were refused service. They then simply continued to sit at the counter in protest—notwithstanding cursing, pushing, spitting, and catsup-throwing by their white neighbors. Ultimately, the four filed out, formed a tight circle on the sidewalk, recited the Lord's Prayer—and another group took over for them inside.

This example of non-violent protest spread to six more North Carolina and forty-eight other cities as well as eight additional Southern states within four weeks. Not only did the Greensboro sit-in set a precedent, it led directly to the organization of the aforementioned Student Non-violent Co-

---

[234] As quoted by Martin Luther King, Jr., "Letter From Birmingham Jail," in *Why We Can't Wait* (New York: Harper and Row, 1963), p. 99.

[235] *Gayle v. Browder*, 352 U.S. 903 (1956).

[236] Joseph McNeil, David Richmond, Franklin McCain, and Ezell Blair, Jr. (who later changed his name to Jibreel Khazan). Exactly twenty years to the day later (February 1, 1980) the four met triumphantly at the same counter to commemorate the historic event—which was widely covered by the media. A plaque on a downtown street near the site reads:

> SIT-INS
> Launched the national
> drive for integrated
> lunch counters, Feb. 1, 1960,
> in Woolworth
> store 2 blocks south.

ordinating Committee. SNCC quickly began to serve both in the South and in the North as an organizer and backer for "sit-ins" and a large variety of other "ins," such as "stand-ins," "read-ins," "pray-ins," "wade-ins," "sleep-ins," and "lie-ins."[237] Thousands who had never before taken an active part in the protest movement now joined. Variously successful, the movement also gave rise to an intricate set of legal problems stemming from the action by the protesters themselves or by the local authorities who, either by request or on their own initiative, would often arrest the "ins" for such common law offenses as "breach of the peace" or "trespassing." When *statutes* compelling, permitting, or forbidding segregation were present, the legal setting was tailor-made for litigation, of course. But when the actions of the "ins" constituted action against *private* inhospitable hosts acting in their *private* capacity, line-drawing would naturally be far more difficult; here, indeed, the Supreme Court's usually unanimous opinion on race discrimination issues would be bitterly split.

Other participants in "ins" movements, mounted largely by CORE, were the "freedom riders." Their chief target was transportation, supposedly de-segregated for some time. The "rides" not only pinpointed but actually tested, often at the cost of imprisonment and violence, the still prevalent segregation practices in almost all interstate travel and terminal facilities in the deep South. In general, these rides accomplished their purpose: the exposure of continued, rampant violation of what was now the declared law of the land.

The Birmingham Trigger. Yet it was Birmingham, Alabama, that was destined to become the center of the militant black activism of April–May 1963, with vast implications for the years to follow. Having failed to make

---

[237] The developing record of sit-in demonstrations in Southern cities during the fourteen months from February 1, 1960, to March 27, 1961, was as follows (adapted from the special report of the Southern Regional Council, *The Freedom Ride,* published in Atlanta in May 1961):

			DEMONSTRATORS	ARRESTS
Feb. 1, 1960	North Carolina	Greensboro	4,200	268
Feb. 11	Virginia	Hampton	11,000	235
Feb. 12	South Carolina	Rock Hill	4,000	947
Feb. 12	Florida	Deland	2,500	243
Feb. 13	Tennessee	Nashville	16,000	692
Feb. 25	Alabama	Montgomery	5,500	86
Feb. 27	Kentucky	Lexington	6,000	374
March 5	Texas	Houston	6,500	317
March 10	Arkansas	Little Rock	50	20
March 15	Georgia	Atlanta	7,000	292
March 28	Louisiana	Baton Rouge	10,000	71
March 27, 1961	Mississippi	Jackson	1,600	40
		Totals	74,350	3,585

For further illustrative aspects of the matter see Table 4, "Peaceful Rights Demonstrations, 1954–1968," in Jonathan W. Casper, *The Politics of Civil Liberties* (New York: Harper and Row, 1972), p. 90.

headway in the quest for desegregation in the state's largest and most highly industrialized city, mass street demonstrations, involving thousands, including school children, were staged there by Dr. King and his faithful allies, the Reverends Ralph D. Abernathy and Fred L. Shuttlesworth. Some 150 demonstrators were arrested on the first day, but the protests continued with a march and a "kneel-in" in the face of a court injunction. When the three leaders were also arrested, the street demonstrations daily grew larger. So did the prison populace, reaching 2,500 in a matter of days. Failing to obtain any concessions, the blacks continued to demonstrate, and were now met by high-pressure water hoses, police dogs, and cattle-prods. The entire nation was outraged, and the Birmingham authorities, under pressure from both the Kennedy Administration and local business leaders, agreed to a "truce," promising alleviation of black grievances in public accommodation, employment opportunities, and interracial commit-tees. But Governor Wallace promptly denounced the agreement, and on May 11, after a series of bomb blasts directed against, among others, Dr. King and his brother, thousands of irate blacks resumed demonstrations. ours the streets were filled with uncontrollable rioters battling with ice. At this juncture President Kennedy, having experienced nothing defiance from Wallace, dispatched 3,000 federal troops to the area— ut not to Birmingham itself. This seemed to achieve results; racial ten-sions gradually subsided. And although they were revived by Governor Wallace's infamous "schoolhouse door stand," which unsuccessfully tried to prevent the court-ordered admission of two blacks to the University of Alabama at Tuscaloosa, an important corner had been turned. After Wallace's interference with court-ordered desegregation of certain public schools was blocked by the federalization of the Alabama National Guard that September, a tenuous peace finally came to Birmingham. Tragically it did so only after four little black girls had died in the wreckage of the bombed Sixteenth Street Baptist Church and two black teenagers had been gunned down by white terrorists.

These 1963 events set off chain reactions throughout the country. In the seventy days following the Birmingham "truce," almost 800 racial demon-strations took place in the nation. They culminated in the mammoth, or-derly Washington march of August 1963, in which, as already noted, more than 200,000 blacks and whites participated. Racial demonstrations con-tinued during the ensuing six summers throughout Northern cities.[238] Not even the new federal civil rights and voting statutes would lessen the now determined, often militant and impatient drive for black equality. It had obtained results! For most Southerners and, indeed increasingly, North-

---

[238] See pp. 311–12, *supra,* for statistics and details. Few, if any, of the large centers, were spared.

erners as well, adaptation to change had become a fact of daily life for
state and local governments; racial incidents had to be avoided; and resistance to federal authority was, in the long run, futile. Still, the Southern
leadership was allowed to move slowly and, with some exceptions, to do
nothing more than the bare minimum. "Tokenism" was still the rule of
the day.

This attitude, however understandable it might be in terms of the practices and traditions of generations, continued to incite militancy on the
part of the increasingly restive blacks—and now particularly those in the
ghettos of the *Northern* cities. They were tired of waiting, tired of gradualism, tired of tokenism. In effect, they demanded what was patently impossible: full equality "here and now"—and if that meant "favored treatment,"
so be it! But black poverty, both of means and of opportunity, and prejudice—always prejudice—could not be eradicated so quickly. The resultant
frustration frequently generated overt belligerency, often referred to by the
participants as "direct action," which was frequently, although by no means
inevitably, counter-productive to the aims of the black cause and wh
indicated, provoked a serious split in the Supreme Court,[239] whic
fore had been supporting civil rights causes with unanimity.

While it is feasible to offer explanations for the wave of question
and tragic actions, such as the riots that swept so many Northern cit
between 1963 and 1969, there could be no excuse for the looting, the burn-
ing, the destruction, the loss of lives—the reckless dedication to manifesta-
tions of hate. As a result, there was mounting fear among civil rights leaders and supporters that the days of wide national support for civil rights
had come to an end, at least temporarily. It would ultimately prove to be
a groundless fear, but the failure of Congress to pass the 1966 Civil Rights
bill seemed to confirm it at the time. And as President Johnson—who had
done so much for blacks—told a group of visiting bishops from the all-
black African Methodist Episcopal Church in October of that year:

> We have entered a new phase. . . . What if the cry for freedom becomes
> the sound of a brick cracking through a store window, turning over an
> automobile in the street, or the sound of the mob? If that sound should
> drown out the voices of reason, frustration will replace progress and all of
> our best work will be undone.[240]

In any event, it was now clear that, even in the non-violent sector of
black protest, lines were becoming increasingly blurred: had not the limits
of civil disobedience in a free representative democracy now been reached,

[239] See, among others, *Bell v. Maryland,* 378 U.S. 226 (1964); *Hamm v. City of Rock Hill,* 379 U.S. 306 (1964); *Elton v. Cox,* 379 U.S. 536 (1965); *Brown v. Louisiana,* 383 U.S. 131 (1966); *Adderley v. Florida,* 385 U.S. 39 (1966); and *Cameron v. Johnson,* 390 U.S. 611 (1968).

[240] As quoted in *Time,* October 7, 1966, p. 17.

and sometimes exceeded? There is a difference between the exercise of constitutional rights that are inherent in the freedoms of speech, press, assembly, and petition and the kind of militant, often lawless, activities that were becoming frequent. The basic issues of racial discrimination, of the injustices of generations, were obvious; there could no longer be any doubt of the need for the acknowledgment, both legally and morally, of full egalitarianism. Yet, it was also obvious that it would still take a long time to achieve it in the public sphere—and it would take infinitely longer in the *private* sector.

Since the means of amelioration of injustice in a representative democracy are patently lodged in the public sector, one of the great issues of the day thus became: just what constitutes that "public" sphere, which *is* reachable by the authority of government under law? Just when does an action become "state action"—an action subject to the commands and sanctions of the Constitution, in general, and Amendment Fourteen, in particular?

State Action and Beyond: A True Dilemma

The words of the famed second sentence of Section 1 of the Fourteenth Amendment concerning "state action" would seem to be quite clear:

> *No State shall make or enforce any law* which shall abridge the privileges or immunities of citizens of the United States; *nor shall any State deprive* any person of life, liberty, or property without due process of law; *nor deny to any person within its jurisdiction the equal protection of the laws.*[241]

What is proscribed here is *discriminatory state action* only; it does *not* extend to *private action* (unless, of course, it has been legislatively covered to extend to the private sector—as is significantly true, for example, of segments of the Civil Rights Acts of 1964 and 1968 and their progeny). And this is the interpretation the judiciary has quite naturally and appropriately given to the Amendment. But at what point has a State, or its "agent," deprived an individual of life, liberty, or property without due process of law; or, more appropriately since black litigants have relied predominantly upon the "equal protection of the laws" clause, when has a State, or its "agent," denied an individual that equal protection? The important question is not so much "state action" *per se,* but whether, as Court opinions have demonstrated increasingly, "state action" denies "equal protection."

THE DILEMMA

Technically, *state action* is any action taken by legislative, executive, or judicial instrumentalities of the state. *Private action* is any act or action en-

[241] Italics supplied.

gaged in or perpetrated by any individual in his private capacity and association.[242] But six Supreme Court justices in a highly significant set of racial violence cases in 1966,[243] warned that they would feel bound to uphold any appropriate law aimed at punishing *private* individuals who use violence to deny persons their Fourteenth Amendment rights. Of course, *state* activity causing or abetting racial discrimination would, under present-day interpretations by the courts, be regarded as patently violating the Fourteenth Amendment injunctions against discriminatory state action. It is thus that the "separate but equal" concept met its doom, along with the manifold instances of state-authored or state-enforced racial discrimination in education, transportation, housing, employment, voting, and a vast array of other areas. But *private* discrimination, or so it might be assumed, would be entirely legal, even though neither democratic nor just. Hence, until the passage of the federal Civil Rights Act of 1964, it was not considered illegal to refuse to serve or admit blacks in privately owned establishments, such as restaurants, hotels, motels, or theaters, so long as the owner was *really* a *private* person, acting in his *private* capacity, and, of course, provided that *state* law did not forbid such discrimination.

Even before the Civil Rights Act of 1964 extended the reach of governmental proscription of discrimination on racial, religious, ethnic and other related grounds to such contentious areas as public accommodations and employment, however, the distinction between "public" and "private" under certain conditions had been legally questioned, although never really effectively challenged. Perhaps the first such instance to raise and at the same time to befuddle the basic issue at the bar of the judiciary was the *Restrictive Covenant* decision, *Shelley v. Kraemer*.[244] Briefly, in the lead case, J. D. and Ethel Lee Shelley, black citizens from St. Louis, Missouri, had "for valuable consideration" received in 1945 from one Josephine Fitzgerald a warranty deed to a parcel of land situated in an area restricted by common agreement of some thirty resident-owners to persons of "the Caucasian race." The restrictive covenant, originally scheduled to run from

---

[242] One expert, Professor Louis Henkin, suggests three bases for holding the state legally responsible *when private discrimination is involved:* (1) "The state is responsible for what it could prevent, and should prevent, and fails to prevent." (2) "The state is responsible for discrimination which it encourages or sanctions." (3) "The state is responsible when its courts act to render discrimination effective." See his *"Shelley v. Kraemer:* Notes for a Revised Opinion," 110 *University of Pennsylvania Law Review* 481–87 (February 1962). Yet some of his arguments in this important and scholarly article would seem to cast doubt on his own tests.

[243] *United States v. Price,* 383 U.S. 688 (1966); and *United States v. Guest,* 383 U.S. 746 (1966). Expressed in two concurring opinions, severally joined by Mr. Chief Justice Warren and Associate Justices Black, Douglas, Clark, Brennan, and Fortas. *Griffin v. Breckenridge,* 403 U.S. 88 (1971) unanimously confirmed and expanded the two earlier holdings via Amendment Thirteen.

[244] 334 U.S. 1 (1948). A similar question was raised by a Detroit group and was decided concurrently.

1911 to 1961, specifically barred "people of the Negro or Mongolian race." Louis and Fern E. Kraemer, for the restrictive covenanters, attempted to block the Fitzgerald-to-Shelley sale in the appropriate Missouri State Circuit Court, but they lost—more or less on an interpretative technicality. The Supreme Court of Missouri, however, reversed the lower court's ruling and directed it to order the Shelleys to vacate their property.

Yet with Justices Reed, Jackson, and Rutledge taking no part in either the consideration or the decision of the case, the Supreme Court of the United States unanimously *reversed* the highest Missouri tribunal. Speaking through Mr. Chief Justice Vinson, the Court affirmed that orders by state courts *enforcing* restrictive covenants based on race and color are violative of the "equal protection of the laws" clause of the Fourteenth Amendment. Restrictive covenants drawn up by private individuals, reasoned the Court, are not in themselves a violation of the Amendment's commands so long as they are completely private and voluntary, and, of course, do not breach some federal or state law or state ordinance (which restrictive covenants in the housing field would have done in a number of states even in the late 1940s; and since the enactment of the federal fair housing law of 1968 and the Supreme Court's decision in *Jones v. Alfred H. Mayer Co.*,[245] such covenants would be illegal anywhere in the country). "Here, however," the Chief Justice pointed out, "there was more," because the State of Missouri, through its judicial branch, not only *aided in the enforcement* of the restrictive covenant—which would in itself have constituted forbidden state action—but, in effect, rendered the agreements workable. "We have no doubt," concluded America's highest jurist, "that there has been *state action* in the full and complete sense of the phrase."[246]

In other words, *Shelley* presented the intriguing dichotomy of permitting private discrimination so long as no state aid in its implementation or enforcement was sought: the judicial aid desired by Kraemer and his supporters *was* regarded as such state aid. The implications of the *Shelley* case became quickly apparent, and the decision evoked a flood of favorable, unfavorable, and tentative commentary by laymen and professionals alike.[247] But whatever one's feelings regarding either the equity of the decision or the viability of the dichotomy it enunciated, the decision brought the state action problem to the fore. In brief, the problem comes down to

[245] 392 U.S. 409 (1968). See the discussion regarding the statute and the *Mayer* decision on p. 352, *supra*, and p. 384, *infra*.

[246] *Shelley v. Kraemer, op. cit.*, at 13, 19.

[247] For example, Herbert Wechsler, "Toward Neutral Principles of Constitutional Law," 73 *Harvard Law Review* 1 (1959); Louis Henkin, "Some Reflections on Current Constitutional Controversy," 109 *University of Pennsylvania Law Review* 637 (1961); Henkin, "*Shelley v. Kraemer*: Notes for a Revised Opinion," *op. cit.*; and Louis Pollak, "Racial Discrimination and Judicial Integrity: A Reply to Professor Wechsler," 108 *University of Pennsylvania Law Review* 1 (1959).

the crucial question of a free democratic society: how to reconcile the competing rights and claims of *equality and liberty*—a question as old as the ages. Where *does* the Constitution draw the line between the right to legal equality and to equality of opportunity, and the rights of liberty, property,[248] privacy, and voluntary association? Where *do* we draw it? Where *should* we draw it? Where *can* we draw it? It is, of course, a balancing problem. Yet "balancing" is a delicate matter, often regarded as "nasty," even unconstitutional in some quarters—particularly when applied to the Bill of Rights. Thus, notwithstanding his avowedly absolutist position on the First Amendment,[249] Mr. Justice Black was deeply disturbed over the implications of the broad interpretation of "state action" under the Fourteenth Amendment; in fact, he came to "balance" *here*—most notably in some of the sit-in and demonstration cases[250] although he did *not* in the cases concerning the First Amendment. A few additional illustrations of the problem of private and state action and rights may be helpful (although it ought to be noted that the problem is assuredly not confined to matters of race).

Popular Referenda and State Action. The housing field provides a number of fascinatingly complex state action cases—particularly when "state action" involves a linkage to what, presumably, is *the* most democratic expression of a free participating electorate: the "direct democracy" instrumentalities of initiative and/or the referendum. What if a state's electorate, in a free and open election, approves a constitutional amendment to a state constitution, duly initiated by that state's electorate, that was designed to repeal fair housing legislation previously passed by the state legislature? This is precisely what occurred in the case of "Proposition 14" in California in 1964, when that state's voters, by the almost 2:1 margin of 4.5 to 2.4 million votes, adopted the following seemingly neutral provision: "Neither the state nor any subdivision or agency thereof shall deny . . . the right of any person . . . to decline to sell, lease, or rent [real] property to such person or persons as he, in his absolute discretion, chooses." Approved by an overwhelming majority, the provision became Section 26 of the California Constitution. *But* when a challenge to the newly adopted provision reached the California Supreme Court in 1966, that tribunal ruled it unconstitutional (5:2) as a violation of the "equal protection of the laws" clause of the Fourteenth Amendment, reasoning that "when the electorate assumes to exercise the law-making function [as it had done here

[248] In that connection see the interesting 5:4 Supreme Court decision in *San Antonio Independent School District v. Rodriguez,* which dealt, among other things, with the matter of "state action" and "equal protection" regarding the use of the property tax to fund public education (411 U.S. 1 [1973]).

[249] See the explanation and analysis of his position throughout the pages of this book, particularly in Chapters II, III, and V, *passim.*

[250] See p. 370, footnote 239, *supra* and p. 378, footnote 266, *infra.*

by initiating and then approving Proposition 14], then the electorate is as much a state agency as any of its elected officials."[251] This interpretation of the equal protection clause bewildered many observers, and predictably went to the United States Supreme Court—which, by the narrowest of margins, 5:4, upheld the California tribunal. Mr. Justice White's opinion, joined by Mr. Chief Justice Warren, and Justices Douglas, Brennan, and Fortas, held that the amendment went beyond a mere repeal of the state's fair housing legislation and created "a constitutional right to discriminate on racial grounds in the sale and rental of real property."[252] He concluded that, in effect, the electorate's action constituted "state action"—state action that would impermissibly involve the state in private racial discriminations to an unconstitutional degree. In other words, both the state and the federal judiciary rejected the contention that the electorate's action had merely restored *neutrality;* they instead held that the "in his absolute discretion" clause *ipso facto* legislated discrimination. But in an angry dissenting opinion, joined by Justices Black, Clark, and Stewart, Mr. Justice Harlan pronounced Section 26 unquestionably "neutral" and "inoffensive on its face," that the "state action" required to bring the Fourteenth Amendment into operation must be "affirmative and purposeful"; and he warned, in what constitutes an intriguing exhortation of appropriate institutional roles, that:

> By refusing to accept the decision of the people of California, and by contriving a new and ill-defined constitutional concept to allow Federal judicial interference, I think the court has taken to itself powers and responsibilities left elsewhere by the Constitution.[253]

The *Reitman* holding, notwithstanding its far-reaching implications concerning the range of state action under Amendment Fourteen, seemed to leave the door open, however, for straightforward "neutral" repealers of anti-discrimination legislation. Not only did the White opinion so hint, but during oral argument before the Supreme Court, A. L. Wirin, counsel for the Los Angeles chapter of the American Civil Liberties Union, which sponsored the challenge to Proposition 14, conceded during a colloquy with Justices Black and White that a referendum merely repealing California's fair housing statutes would *not* have been unconstitutional.[254] Yet

[251] *Reitman v. Mulkey,* 64 Cal. 2d 529, at 542.

[252] *Reitman v. Mulkey,* 387 U.S. 369 (1967), at 376. For an excellent commentary on the case see R. E. Wolfinger and F. I. Greenstein, "The Repeal of Fair Housing in California: An Analysis of Referendum Voting," LXII *American Political Science Review* 753 (September 1968).

[253] *Reitman v. Mulkey, op. cit.,* at 396.

[254] *The New York Times,* March 22, 1967, p. 1e, and oral argument at the Supreme Court, March 21, 1967.

along came the Court's 1969 decision in *Hunter v. Erickson*,[255] in which it held, with only Mr. Justice Black dissenting, that an Akron, Ohio, charter provision, adopted by the voters in a city-wide referendum—violated the equal protection of the laws clause. That provision not only repealed a "fair housing" law that had been shortly prior thereto enacted by Akron's City Council but, moreover, required that before any fair housing law could be restored to the books, it would have to be readopted *by a referendum vote*.[256] Speaking for the eight-man Court majority, Mr. Justice White reasoned that, by singling out fair housing laws as the only ones subject to such referendum votes—whereas the City Council regularly and routinely legislates on such other housing matters as rent control and urban renewal—the voters of Akron in effect engaged in constitutionally proscribed state action; that the referendum requirement here "makes an explicitly racial classification." The majority denied Black's contention that it had made even a simple repealer impossible—and it not only proved that point in a 1971 case, but it gave Black an opportunity to write the opinion: At issue was the constitutionality of a California referendum law—similar to that of a good many states—permitting a majority of the voters in a community to block the construction of low-cost housing. A lower federal court had declared it unconstitutional as a violation of the equal protection of the laws clause. Mr. Justice Black's majority opinion, joined by Mr. Chief Justice Burger and Justices Harlan, Stewart, and White, reversed (5:3) the decision below, declaring that the thrust of the Fourteenth Amendment was to outlaw legal distinction based on race; that there was no evidence that the California law was aimed at any racial minority; and that this "procedure for democratic decision making gives the people a voice in decisions that would raise their taxes, dilute the tax base, and affect the future development of the community."[257] But the dissenting opinion by Mr. Justice Marshall, joined by his colleagues Brennan and Blackmun, charged that the statute "explicitly singles out low-income persons" for unequal treatment. "It is far too late in the day," the Court's black member noted, "to contend that the 14th Amendment prohibits only racial discrimination; and to me, singling out the poor to bear a burden not placed on any other class of citizens tramples the values that the 14th Amendment was designed to protect."[258] Yet in a 6:3 ruling in 1976 the Court again sustained a referendum requirement—this time that of a city charter provision in Eastlake, Ohio, requiring land use changes to be rati-

---

[255] 393 U.S. 385.

[256] That provision of the charter (§137) required that any ordinance regulating real estate transactions "on the basis of race, color, religion, national origin or ancestry must first be approved by a majority of the electors voting on the question at a regular or general election before said ordinance shall be effective."

[257] *James v. Valtierra*, 402 U.S. 137 (1971), at 143.

[258] *Ibid.*, at 144.

fied by a 55 per cent referendum majority as well as the city council.[259]
And in 1977 it held (5:3) that it was not inherently unconstitutional for
a suburb to refuse to change zoning restrictions, the practical effect of
which is to block construction of racially integrated housing for persons
with low and moderate income; that to be unconstitutional there must also
be an "intent" or "purpose" to discriminate—which, however, does not
mean that under no circumstances could a village, such as Arlington
Heights, be *statutorily* required to rezone so as to provide such housing.[260]

Aspects of the "In" Syndrome. What of "private" versus "public" action
inherent in the spate of "sit-in" demonstration cases that reached the
Court prior to the Civil Rights Act of 1964?[261] The Act settled the matter
in terms of the constitutionality of the pertinent section, based on congressional power over interstate commerce, *provided* the establishment concerned came under the provisions of the statute governing "public accommodations"; but did it really settle the problem of liberty versus equality
in philosophical terms? Mr. Justice Black had joined in the unanimous
opinion in the two late 1964 cases upholding the law's public accommodations section,[262] yet obviously he did so only because he believed Congress
to have had the power to legislate as it had *because* it *expressly* invoked its
authority over interstate commerce. But, as he had noted orally from the
bench in conjunction with his dissenting opinion in one of the sit-in cases
a few months earlier in 1964, "this Court has never said, in the school segregation decisions or any before or since, that the prejudice of individuals
could be laid to the state."[263] And again, from the bench on the last day of
the Court's 1963–64 term, Black commented that the idea that the Fourteenth Amendment *itself* prohibited segregation in public accommodations
made "the last six months' struggle in Congress a work of supererroga-
tion"[264]—a reference to the prolonged debate that preceded passage of the
legislation. As his long-time jurisprudential "adversary," the retired Mr.
Justice Frankfurter, had done so often, Black then again admonished his
country that: "The worst citizen no less than the best is entitled to equal
protection of the laws of his state and of his nation."[265] And it was Black

---

[259] *Eastlake v. Forest City Enterprises, Inc.,* 426 U.S. 668.

[260] *Village of Arlington Heights v. Metropolitan Housing Development Corp.,* 429
U.S. 252.

[261] For example, *Edwards v. South Carolina,* 372 U.S. 229 (1963); *Peterson v.
Greenville,* 373 U.S. 244 (1963); *Lombard v. Louisiana,* 373 U.S. 267 (1963);
Griffin v. Maryland, 378 U.S. 130 (1964); *Robinson v. Florida,* 378 U.S. 153 (1964);
Barr v. City of Columbia, 378 U.S. 146 (1964); and *Bell v. Maryland,* 378 U.S.
226 (1964).

[262] *Heart of Atlanta Motel v. United States,* 379 U.S. 241 (1964) and *Katzenbach
v. McClung,* 379 U.S. 294 (1964).

[263] *Barr v. City of Columbia, op. cit.,* June 23, 1964.

[264] As quoted in *The New York Times,* June 23, 1964, p. 16*l.*

[265] *Bell v. Maryland,* 378 U.S. 226 (1964), dissenting opinion, at 328.

again, this time joined by Harlan, Stewart, and White, who, having all voted to uphold the constitutionality of the contentious provision of the Civil Rights Act of 1964, took pains to emphasize on the very same Opinion Monday what should be obvious to all believers in law, order, justice, and the dignity of liberty: that the passage of the Act did *not* authorize persons "who are unlawfully refused service a 'right' to take the law into their own hands by sitting down and occupying the premises for as long as they choose to stay."[266] Black's deep concern—one steeped in his high dedication to what he regarded as the prerogatives of home privacy and local control—continued to make itself known, albeit in the minority. Yet he carried three other justices—Clark, Harlan, and Stewart—with him when, in a public library "stand-in" case in 1966, he asked impassionedly:

> Can any provision of the United States Constitution tell any citizens—white or colored—they can march with impunity into a public library and demonstrate against some public policy? . . . It has become automatic for people to be turned loose as long as whatever they do has something to do with race. That is not the way I read the Constitution.[267]

A few pages earlier he had vigorously challenged the majority's position with the exhortation that:

> It is high time to challenge the assumption in which too many people have too long acquiesced, that groups that think they have been mistreated have a constitutional right to use the public streets, buildings, and property to protest whatever, wherever, whenever they want, without regard to whom such conduct may disturb.[268]

That spring the Court summarily *upheld* the conviction of twenty-five New York City racial demonstrators at a housing project[269] and the conviction of a CORE "stand-in" at the office of the police chief of Syracuse.[270] And on the last day of the 1965–66 term, Mr. Justice Clark formally provided the fifth vote for that point of view, and thus a Court majority. He joined his colleagues Black, Harlan, Stewart, and White in holding that twenty-nine persons arrested on various local charges arising from civil rights movements in 1964 in Leflore County, Mississippi, could not have their trials transferred from state to federal courts merely upon their contention that their rights of free speech might be infringed by prejudicial treatment in state courts.[271]

[266] *Hamm v. City of Rock Hill,* 379 U.S. 306 (1964), dissenting opinion, at 318.
[267] *Brown v. Louisiana,* 383 U.S. 131 (1966), dissenting opinion, at 168.
[268] *Ibid.,* at 162.
[269] *Penn v. New York,* 383 U.S. 969 (1966).
[270] *Baer v. New York,* 384 U.S. 154 (1966).
[271] *Greenwood v. Peacock,* 384 U.S. 808 (1966).

Lest that decision be regarded as a procedural "fluke" or one based on a wavering majority, the same five justices again agreed late in 1966 in a case of particular significance in the fundamental freedom-versus-order clash because the civil rights demonstrations involved were directed against *public* rather than *private* property. Speaking through Mr. Justice Black, the five-man majority upheld the "willful-trespass" conviction of Harriet Adderley and thirty-one other Florida A & M University Negro students who had demonstrated outside the Leon County jail in Tallahassee, Florida.[272] The earlier decisions had involved prosecutions for *breach of the peace* rather than trespass. In attempting to draw the line between speech and *conduct*, Black wrote[273]

[N]othing in the Constitution of the United States, prevents Florida from even-handed enforcement of its general trespassing statute against those refusing to obey the sheriff's order to remove themselves. . . . *The state, no less than a private owner of property, has power to preserve the property under its control for the use to which it is lawfully dedicated.*[274]

But to Mr. Justice Douglas, dissenting in a vigorously worded opinion in which he was joined by Warren, Brennan, and Fortas, the Black holding represented "a great break with the traditions of the Court." Now, he said, trespass laws could be used as a "blunderbuss" to suppress civil rights; the Court has, he concluded, "now set into the record a great and wonderful police-state doctrine."[275] Although two subsequent decisions intensified the concern voiced by Douglas and his supporting colleagues,[276] the Court unanimously made clear in 1968 that it is unconstitutional for tribunals to delay public meetings—even when violence is threatened—without hearing testimony from those who wish to meet; that, in other words, there could be no *ex parte* injunctions.[277] And, also unanimously, it reversed in 1969 the 1965 conviction of civil rights leaders King and Shuttlesworth for parading without a permit in Birmingham in 1963 because that city's ordinance gave its commissioners "unfettered discretion" to reject permits.[278] Moreover, in a 1972 decision (*not* involving race) the Court unanimously declared unconstitutional a federal 1882 law that banned all "un-

---

[272] *Adderley v. Florida*, 385 U.S. 39 (1966). The Florida statute reads: "Every trespass on the property of another, committed with a malicious and mischievous intent . . . shall be punished."

[273] See his discussion of that vexatious line in his *A Constitutional Faith* (New York: Alfred A. Knopf, 1968), pp. 53–56.

[274] *Adderley v. Florida, op. cit.,* at 47. (Italics supplied.)

[275] *Ibid.,* extemporaneous remark from the bench, November 14, 1966.

[276] *Walker v. Birmingham*, 388 U.S. 307 (1967) and *Cameron v. Johnson*, 390 U.S. 611 (1968).

[277] *Carroll v. President and Commissioners of Princess Anne County*, 393 U.S. 175.

[278] *Shuttlesworth v. Birmingham*, 394 U.S. 147.

authorized" demonstrations on the grounds of the United States capitol.[279] Clearly, then, the line is drawn on the basis of each case's facts.

State Action or Routine Service? What of such services rendered by the state as *licensing* or the *probation of wills* that do involve the state, but which had heretofore been regarded as *routine services* rather than as state action? If these services were to be construed as "state action," would not almost *everything* then be state action? Would anything remain in the private sphere at all?

Girard College. The matter of probation of discriminatory wills (of which there are innumerable examples) underwent its first important post-*Brown* litigation in the *Girard College* cases,[280] involving Philadelphia's famed Girard College (actually a private elementary and high school for "male, white orphans" as provided in the generous will of Stephen S. Girard, an early 19th-century Philadelphia merchant). The trust established by Girard's will was being administered by the Board of Directors of the City of Philadelphia when in 1957 the Supreme Court of the United States, citing the precedent of the *Public School Segregation Cases,*[281] ruled unconstitutional as a violation of the "equal protection of the laws" clause of Amendment Fourteen the municipality's described participation in the Girard trust's administration.[282] It was deemed "state action." But then an interesting turn of events took place: the Board of Directors of City Trusts asked the Orphans Court—the appropriate tribunal of jurisdiction—to *remove the municipal trustees* and to *substitute private trustees.* This the Orphans Court promptly did, and the Supreme Court of Pennsylvania upheld the action as not being violative of the equal protection clause's "state action" concept. In other words, the state judiciary did not regard either the administration of the trust by private individuals or the role of the two courts in facilitating it to be constitutionally proscribed. On the Pennsylvania Attorney-General's petition for a writ of *certiorari,* the United States Supreme Court denied review,[283] thus upholding the state tribunals.

The Girard issue continued to bubble, however, and became acute again fully eight years later when, following lengthy sparring between the NAACP and the school's board of trustees, U.S. District Court Judge Joseph S. Lord, III, ruled that blacks could not be excluded from Girard College

---

[279] *Chief of Capitol Police v. Jeannette Rankin Brigade,* 409 U.S. 972.

[280] *Pennsylvania v. Board of Directors of City Trusts of the City of Philadelphia,* 353 U.S. 230 (1957) and 357 U.S. 570 (1958), *certiorari* denied. (These two citations are confined to *Supreme Court* action. There was a host of lower federal and state case dispositions, of course.)

[281] *Brown v. Board of Education of Topeka,* 347 U.S. 483 (1954).

[282] *Pennsylvania v. Board of Directors of City Trusts of the City of Philadelphia,* 353 U.S. 230.

[283] *Ibid.,* 357 U.S. 570 (1958).

under Pennsylvania law. Specifically *refusing to pass on the probate problem,* Judge Lord simply held that the Pennsylvania Public Accommodations Act of 1939—which threw open all *public* institutions and accommodations—applied to Girard College, for he classified it as a "public institution."[284] Shortly thereafter, he ordered the admission of seven black orphans if they were otherwise found to qualify.[285] The trustees appealed his decision to the U.S. Third Circuit Court of Appeals which first stayed Judge Lord's order and then reversed him on the grounds that the 1939 statute did *not* apply to Girard College.[286] The plaintiffs, armed with a different strategy, returned to Judge Lord in 1967. The latter, eschewing the Pennsylvania law as well as any probation of wills consideration, now ruled that Girard's refusal to admit the black applicants constituted a violation of the "equal protection of the laws" clause by virtue of being proscribable *state action* under the Constitution, since the College was sufficiently "public" (e.g., tax exempt) to invoke the Fourteenth Amendment's state action strictures.[287] This time the United States Court of Appeals, in a three-opinion 5:0 decision, affirmed Judge Lord's ruling. The principal opinion, written by Judge Gerald McLaughlin, turned predominantly on the quasi-public nature of the institution—which constituted sufficient "state action."[288] The Supreme Court refused to review,[289] and thus another attempt to make distinctions in the realm of racial discrimination sector had succeeded. But could the distinction hold? What of "private" parks, deeded in a bequest, for example?

Bacon's Park. The Court soon confronted the question of whether such a privately owned park, here one in Macon, Georgia, could discriminate racially because of the terms of the original donor's will. In 1914, the 100-acre park had been left in trust to the City of Macon by the will of a former Confederate general, Senator Augustus Octavius Bacon, stipulating that the park's use be reserved for "white women and children." As did parts of the Girard will, Bacon's bequest contained a number of features that were ultimately branded as "state action" by civil rights leaders. The will had been drawn up under a Georgia law that, unlike Pennsylvania's, *specifically permitted segregation* in charitable trusts. But like Philadelphia, Macon appointed the trustees and, like Girard College, Bacon's Park was considered an eleemosynary institution and therefore tax exempt.

---

[284] *Commonwealth of Pennsylvania v. Brown,* 260 F. Supp. 323 (1966).
[285] *Commonwealth of Pennsylvania v. Brown,* 360 F. Supp. 358 (1966).
[286] *Ibid.,* 373 F. 2d 771 (1967).
[287] *Ibid.,* 270 F. Supp. 782 (1967).
[288] *Ibid.,* 392 F. 2d 120 (1968).
[289] *Brown v. Commonwealth of Pennsylvania,* 391 U.S. 921 (1968). For an engaging, albeit not unflawed, summary of the *Girard* case (and the eccentric Stephen S. Girard) see John Keats, "Legacy of Stephen Girard," 29 *American Heritage* 38 (June/July 1978).

Similar to the Philadelphia actions regarding Girard, Macon withdrew as trustee in 1963 and transferred the fiduciary authority to private trustees after lower federal courts had ruled unmistakably that a municipality could not constitutionally operate a segregated park.

Six blacks, successful in getting the trustee transfer question before the Supreme Court, contended that Macon had become so intimately involved in the operations of Bacon's Park that to permit private individuals to take over and continue to discriminate racially would be tantamount to "unconstitutional state action." In a 6:3 decision, with Mr. Justice Douglas delivering the Court's opinion, the Supreme Court agreed with the six petitioners.[290] It held that Macon had become so "entwined" in the park's operation that the mere change of trustees could not constitutionally remove the command to desegregate. Joined by the Chief Justice, and Associate Justices Brennan, Clark, and Fortas, Douglas held that park services are "municipal in nature" and in the "public domain." Under the circumstances, he ruled, "we cannot but conclude that the public character of this park requires that it be treated as a public institution" and therefore subject to the commands of the "equal protection of the laws" clause of the Fourteenth Amendment. As opposed to golf clubs, social centers, *private schools,*[291] and other similar organizations, a park, Douglas explained, "is more like a fire department or police department that traditionally serves the community. Mass recreation through the use of parks is plainly in the public domain."[292]

Justices Harlan and Stewart dissented, as did Black, but the latter did so on separate and largely jurisdictional grounds. To Harlan and Stewart, the Douglas contention was at best dubious. Noting that Douglas had specifically excepted private schools, Harlan was nonetheless alarmed, contending that the Douglas theory could "be spun out to reach *privately owned* orphanages, libraries, garbage collection companies, detective agencies, and a host of other functions *commonly regarded as nongovernmental though paralleling fields of governmental activity.*"[293] As for private schools, Harlan argued cogently that the "public function" of privately established schools and privately established parks is assuredly similar. If, Harlan continued, the majority really believed that its ruling left "unaffected the traditional view that the Fourteenth Amendment does *not* compel private schools to adapt their admission policies to its requirements," he certainly could not agree with their interpretation in the light of the *Bacon's Park* case. He regarded it as indeed difficult

---

[290] *Evans v. Newton,* 382 U.S. 296 (1966).
[291] See the discussion of burgeoning private school developments in 1976, pp. 388–92, *infra.*
[292] *Ibid.,* at 302.
[293] *Ibid.,* at 322. (Italics supplied.)

to avoid the conclusion that this decision opens the door to reversal of these basic constitutional concepts. . . . The example of schools is, I think, sufficient to indicate the pervasive potentialities of this "public function" theory . . . a catch phrase as vague and amorphous as it is far-reaching.[294]

But, in one of those unpredictable Court actions, the Supreme Court ruled (5:2) four years later that Baconsfield (as Senator Bacon had called it) could be returned to the donor's heirs despite a federal court order to admit blacks to its use.[295] In thus siding with the Georgia Supreme Court, Mr. Justice Black—speaking also for Mr. Chief Justice Burger, and Justices Harlan, Stewart, and White—concluded that no constitutionally forbidden state action was involved here; that the Georgia courts had merely carried out Senator Bacon's wishes and had not themselves acted to discriminate against Macon's blacks; and that the Fourteenth Amendment's crucial equal protection of the laws clause had not therefore been violated. Dissenting, Justices Brennan and Douglas, however, asserted that making the park private to frustrate desegregation *did* amount to discriminatory state action.[296] In any event, at least as of this writing (mid-1981)—and buttressed by a 1975 holding, with only Mr. Justice Douglas in dissent[297]—it seems clear that the mere probation of a will falls outside the realm of the kind of "state action" governed by constitutional commands—which is not to say that a future Court may not read the Constitution differently.

Jackson's Pool. Demonstrating its capability of "surprises" and the dangers of attempting predictions as to its course of action, the Court, dividing 5:4, held in a contentious 1971 Mississippi litigation that public officials may close all of a city's public swimming pools rather than comply with a court order to desegregate them—the city having desegregated its public parks, golf courses, auditoria, and the City Zoo.[298] Thus the majority opinion, written by Mr. Justice Black—who was joined by his colleagues Harlan, Stewart, Blackmun, and Mr. Chief Justice Burger—upheld the right of the City Council of Jackson to shut its five community pools on the claimed grounds that to integrate them would be "uneconomical" and create a threat of violence. Refusing to be drawn into attempts to "ascertain the motivation, or collection of different motivations, that lie behind a legislative enactment," Black ruled:

[294] *Ibid.,* at 322.

[295] *Evans v. Abney,* 396 U.S. 435 (1970).

[296] The Court's sole black member, Mr. Justice Thurgood Marshall, disqualified himself from sitting in the case because he was once chief counsel for the NAACP Legal Defense and Educational Fund, Inc., which represented the blacks who began legal proceedings challenging the segregated park in 1963.

[297] *Sutt v. First National Bank of Kansas City,* 421 U.S. 992. The Court here let stand a bequest to Protestant Christian hospitals in a single county to help care for native-born, white patients.

[298] *Palmer v. Thompson,* 403 U.S. 217.

Neither the 14th Amendment nor any act of Congress purports to impose an affirmative duty on a state to begin to operate or to continue to operate swimming pools. . . . It is not a case where a city is maintaining different sets of facilities for blacks and whites and forcing the races to remain separate in recreational or educational activities.[299]

But in his heated dissenting opinion, Mr. Justice White, joined by his colleagues Brennan, Marshall, and Douglas—who also issued a separate one, based on his reading of the Ninth Amendment—accused the majority of turning back the clock seventeen years on racial equality, of adopting a policy tantamount to "apartheid." In White's words, "a State may not have an official stance against desegregating public facilities . . . implemented by closing those facilities in response to a desegregation order."[300] At the least, "an honest difference of opinion about what the Constitution says,"[301] as Black put it, underlay the Court's majority opinion—one replete with broad implications for future policy judgments and decisions (irrespective of the fact that Jackson *voluntarily* reopened its pools on an integrated basis a few years later).

Private Clubs. Perhaps not one of the most important on the scale of basic bread-and-butter values, but assuredly an intriguing one and one replete with considerations of dignity and egalitarianism, as well as freedom of association and liberty, is the matter of the exclusionary policies of private clubs. Even the tough provisions of the Civil Rights Act of 1964, which, among others, forbid places of public accommodation—and these have been broadly defined and construed by the courts[302]—to refuse to discriminate because of race, color, religion, or national origin, leave a specific loophole (in Title II) by *expressly* permitting private clubs to do so, thus testifying to Congress's belief that private clubs can, indeed, discriminate without violating the Constitution. But the courts, of course, are not ultimately bound by the beliefs and/or enactments of Congress, and they have been faced increasingly with difficult questions. When is a "club" a club, i.e., when is a "club" a place of public entertainment rather than a private club exempt under the C.R.A.? At what point, if at all, do the prerogatives the Court "found" in the Civil Rights Act of 1866 as of its 1968 fair-housing law decision[303] vitiate prevailing concepts of the rights of private clubs? And, finally, and most importantly, at what point, if any, does a club's actions, and the services it receives, constitute proscribable "state

---

[299] *Ibid.,* at 220.

[300] *Ibid.,* at 240.

[301] *Ibid.* Oral comment from bench, June 14, 1971.

[302] E.g., *Heart of Atlanta Motel v. United States,* 379 U.S. 241 (1964) and *Katzenbach v. McClung,* 379 U.S. 294 (1964). See also pp. 374 ff., *supra.*

[303] *Jones v. Alfred H. Mayer Co.,* 392 U.S. 409 (1964). See p. 385, footnote 307, *infra,* for the Act's key provision on housing. See also the Court's important 1967 *Gautreaux* decision, p. 345, footnote 150, *supra.*

action"? In the 1970s the Supreme Court began to face each of these questions.

Thus, as to when is a "club" a club, the Court ruled (7:1) in 1969 that so-called "private recreational clubs" cannot resort to subterfuge to bar blacks from membership when, in fact, they are *not* private.[304] The case involved a swimming, boating, and picnicking club near Little Rock, Arkansas (Lake Nixon); the establishment widely advertised that it charged but 25 cents for "membership," and had 100,000 "members" in a single year. While the lower federal courts, to whom two excluded blacks had appealed, found the "club" arrangements to be a sham, they held that blacks could nonetheless be excluded because Lake Nixon was a private, local activity, not covered by the Civil Rights Act's public accommodations provision. It took a bit of imaginative stretching, but the Supreme Court, speaking through Mr. Justice Brennan, with only Mr. Justice Black in dissent, found that the establishment *did* affect commerce and therefore came under the statute's reach.[305] How? Well, it solicited business where interstate travelers might respond; it leased canoes from an Oklahoma company; it used a jukebox and records manufactured outside of Arkansas; and ingredients of three out of four items served at the snack bar were shipped interstate. This reasoning was simply too much for Black,[306] but he had no supporters.

In 1969, too, the Court reached the question of whether those provisions of the Civil Rights Act of 1866 which, as explained earlier,[307] outlawed racial discrimination against anyone who wishes to *contract* to buy or lease real estate, extended to any "private club" rights. In a 5:3 decision, written by Mr. Justice Douglas—who was joined by his colleagues Black, Brennan, Marshall, and Stewart, with Justices Harlan, White, and Mr. Chief Justice Burger dissenting—the Court ruled that the 1866 statute prevented the exclusion of a black family, that had moved into a certain neighborhood housing development, from a swimming pool and a park owned by residents of the suburban community involved.[308] The excluded black applicant for membership, Dr. R. Freeman, Jr., an official of the De-

[304] For example, in 1976 the Court upheld a lower tribunal's ruling that health spas are "places of entertainment" within the meaning of the C.R.A. of 1964 and thus subject to the Act's prohibition against racial discrimination. (*Shape Spa for Health & Beauty, Inc. v. Rousseve*, 425 U.S. 911, [1976].)

[305] *Daniel v. Paul*, 395 U.S. 298 (1968).

[306] As he put it: "This would be stretching the commerce clause so as to give the federal government complete control over every little remote country place of recreation in every nook and cranny of every precinct and county in every one of the fifty states. This goes too far for me."

[307] See pp. 352 ff., *supra*. The Act's pertinent provision (42 U.S.C.A. §1982) reads: "All citizens of the United States shall have the same right, in every State and Territory, as is enjoyed by white citizens thereof to inherit, purchase, lease, sell, hold, and convey real and personal property."

[308] *Sullivan v. Little Hunting Park, Inc.*, 396 U.S. 229 (1969).

partment of Agriculture, had obtained a share in the pool and park with the lease of his house from its owner-member, Paul E. Sullivan. Not only did the development's board of directors refuse to admit Dr. Freeman, they also expelled Mr. Sullivan from membership when he protested the action. The Douglas opinion did not decide whether a club membership is "personal property" under the 1866 Act, since the share in the development (Little Hunting Park) was part of the lease itself. The three dissenters objected that the majority unnecessarily propounded grave constitutional questions, that the fair housing provisions of the Civil Rights Act of 1968 would have provided the same relief without reliance upon the vaguely worded 1866 law. The majority left undecided the broader question of whether private clubs that admit white applicants without selectivity may legally exclude blacks when *no* lease is involved—an issue it again dodged, perhaps quite understandably, four years later.[309]

But what of a private club or lodge that discriminates on racial—or, for that matter, on sexual or religious grounds and *holds a state liquor license?* In the absence of "state action," even the tough provisions of the Civil Rights Act of 1964 specifically exempt *private* organizations from its non-discrimination mandates. Is the grant of a state liquor license the sort of "state action" at issue, or is it, like probating of wills, merely a "service" that does not constitute proscribable state action? The judicial response to date has been rather equivocal but, on the whole, the answer would appear to be negative—at least of this writing (mid-1981)—so long as a state (or federal) law does not specifically bar such discrimination as a condition for obtaining either a license or tax exemption.

Thus, could the Loyal Order of Moose, for example, limit membership in its 2,000 lodges to white adult Caucasian males—who, if married, are married to "white Caucasians," and are of "good moral character," "mentally normal," and "express a belief in a supreme being"? If it is a truly private organization, receives no governmental aid, and pays its taxes, the answer would presumably be "yes"—for the liberty to associate privately, even if it be on a discriminatory basis, would appear to outweigh egalitarian commands, especially since the First and Fourteenth Amendments guarantee freedom of association and liberty as well as equality. The Har-

---

[309] Relying heavily on its 1969 decision, the Court, speaking through Mr. Justice Blackmun, held unanimously: "When an organization links membership benefits to residency in a narrow geographical area, that decision infuses those benefits into the bundle of rights for which an individual pays when buying or leasing within the area." *Tillman v. Wheaton-Haven Recreation Association,* 410 U.S. 431 (1973), at 437. The Association drew *all* of its members from *whites* living within three-quarters of a mile from its swimming pool, and barred all *non-whites* living in the same area. The Court refused to recognize the Association as a "private club on any level." See also a similar stance in 1980 by the United States Court of Appeals for the Fourth Circuit, by overturning a lower court ruling that had dismissed a charge of racial discrimination. (*Wright v. Salisbury Country Club, Ltd.,* 632 F. 2d and 479 F. Supp. 378, respectively.)

risburg, Pennsylvania, Lodge #107 of the Moose, possessor of a state liquor license, refused to serve a meal and drinks to K. Leroy Irvis, the black Majority Leader of the Pennsylvania State House of Representatives, who had gone to the Lodge as a guest of a Moose member. Evidently, the Lodge did not discriminate selectively in its discrimination against blacks! After losing in Pennsylvania Commonwealth Court—which called the Lodge's refusal to serve Irvis "morally indefensible and deficient in good manners and common sense,"[310] but held the Lodge to be a private club exempt on grounds of privacy and association[311]—Representative Irvis brought suit before a three-judge Federal District Court, contending that state regulation of liquor was "so detailed and pervasive" that to license a club that discriminated was tantamount to licensing discrimination. Unanimously, the three-judge tribunal ruled in Mr. Irvis's favor, agreeing that the holder of a liquor license was, indeed, clothed with "state action" under the Fourteenth Amendment.[312] Blurring the issues somewhat, however, the court added that the Lodge could continue to discriminate on the basis of religion and national origin—it said nothing about sex—because it did not regard these characteristics to be protected by that Civil War Amendment—which had been adopted primarily to prevent discrimination against blacks.

The Lodge, in its resultant appeal to the U.S. Supreme Court, called that distinction "clearly fallacious," and pointed to the stipulated exemption of private clubs under the public accommodations provision of the Civil Rights Act of 1964. Moreover, it invoked freedom of association concepts under the First (and Fourteenth) Amendment. The high tribunal evidently agreed, at least in part: in a 6:3 opinion, written by Mr. Justice Rehnquist—Justices Douglas, Brennan, and Marshall dissenting—it ruled that *mere liquor regulation* does *not* involve the state in the kind of discriminatory state action forbidden by the Fourteenth Amendment's equal protection clause.[313] However, the *Moose Lodge* decision did *not* mean that states could not make the receipt of a liquor license, or its continued retention, contingent upon the eschewing of racial discrimination—as fifteen Maine "Elk" lodges soon found out.[314] On the other hand, in the absence of state laws prohibiting discrimination on the basis of *sex* as well as race

[310] *Commonwealth v. Loyal Order of Moose,* 92 Dauph. 234 (1970).

[311] *Ibid.,* at 239.

[312] *Irvis v. Scott and Moose Lodge #107,* 318 F. Supp. 1246 (1970), at 1251.

[313] *Moose Lodge #107 v. Irvis,* 407 U.S. 163 (1972). But it ought to be noted, that when—just two months after the Court's decision—the Pennsylvania State Human Relations Commission ruled that Lodge #107 had in fact turned itself into a *"public accommodation"* because it freely allowed guests, and thus could not ban blacks under state law, the State Supreme Court affirmed, and the U.S. Supreme Court dismissed the Lodge's appeal, thus upholding the Commission's ruling. (*Loyal Order of Moose v. Pennsylvania Human Relations Commission,* 409 U.S. 1052 (1972).

[314] *B.P.O.E. Lodge #2043 v. Ingraham,* 412 U.S. 913 (1973). Later that year the Elks dropped their "whites-only" rule.

in places of public accommodation—and in the absence of the adoption of the "Equal Rights Amendment"—the Court has consistently refused to overturn lower tribunal rulings upholding the right of *private* clubs or other *private* organizations that are "male only" to obtain and/or retain liquor licenses.[315] It would seem that, at least as of this writing (mid-1981) the granting of such licenses is in the same category of probation of wills: not sufficiently clothed with "state action" to invoke the strictures of the equal protection of the law clause.[316]

Private Schools. Perhaps the most significant and most emotion-charged area of the "private"–"public" dichotomy, is that of the Fourteenth Amendment "state action" status, if any, of genuinely *private schools.* We know, of course, that those otherwise private institutions of higher and lower learning who receive funds from the federal government, not only have had to toe the proverbial "no discrimination" line in accordance with the mandates of Titles IV, VI, VII, and IX of the Civil Rights Act of 1964, but that the rules laid down by the Departments of Labor, Education, and Health and Human Services have been so adamant and persistent that many aspects of compliance have arguably been justifiably characterized as "reverse discrimination" (of which much more below).[317] But what of the status of governmentally *non*-aided *private* schools? Because they are not covered by the Civil Rights Act of 1964 (and provided they do not fall under state civil rights statutes), may they not, being indeed private, discriminate in their admissions on whatever basis they may determine? In particular, on the basis of race?

That issue reached the highest court in the land in 1976, when it heard oral arguments in the case of *Runyon v. McCrary,* with the nation a fascinated and interested witness. The Court's decision was almost certain to lead to one of the most far-reaching judgments involving the clash between the private and public realms. Involved were two all-white private Virginia

---

[315] E.g., *Millenson v. New Hotel Monteleone,* 414 U.S. 1011 (1973); *Junior Chamber of Commerce of Rochester v. U.S. Jaycees,* 419 U.S. 1026 (1974) and *Junior Chamber of Commerce of Philadelphia v. U.S. Jaycees,* 419 U.S. 1026 (1974). See also the 1977 ruling by federal Judge W. C. Conner, upholding the right of the politically influential Town Club of Scarsdale, New York, to continue to bar women as it has done since 1905 (440 F. Supp. 607). The U.S. Supreme Court also refused to review a lower ruling upholding the right of the international Kiwanis organization to withdraw the charter of an affiliate for having admitted women to its membership. (*Kiwanis Club v. Board of Trustees,* 434 U.S. 859 [1977].) In the same year the Illinois Appellate Court, under Illinois's Liquor Control Act, which specifically sanctions "exclusionary policy" for private clubs, held that private clubs may exclude women and members of minority groups as guests. (*The New York Times,* December 25, 1977, p. A27.)

[316] The tax exemption issue remains murky in this connection: private non-profit fraternal clubs can evidently still enjoy that exemption, even if they discriminate, but all earned income becomes taxable. (*McGlotten v. Connally,* 338 F. Supp. 448, 1972.)

[317] See pp. 396 ff.

schools in the suburbs of Washington, the Fairfax-Brewster School and the Bobbe's School, organized in 1955 and 1958, respectively. Neither had ever admitted a black student. When two black youngsters, Michael McCrary and Colin M. Gonzales, were rejected in 1973, their parents filed suit in federal district court, citing § 1981 of the now more than a century-old Civil Rights Act of 1866, which was enacted to provide for blacks the same right "to make and enforce contracts . . . as is enjoyed by white citizens." Judge Albert V. Bryan, Jr., ruled firmly that private all-white schools cannot legally bar blacks from admission on the basis of race. No "state action" need be shown, he held: the cited provision of the 1866 Civil Rights Act amply covered the quest for redress.[318]

The schools appealed to the United States Circuit Court of Appeals for the Fourth Circuit which, in a 4:3 decision, authored by Mr. Chief Justice Clement F. Haynsworth, Jr.—of 1969 Supreme Court nomination-rejection fame[319]—narrowly affirmed Judge Bryan's holding.[320] A private school, he wrote, "may not refuse with impunity to accept an otherwise qualified black applicant simply because it declines to admit unqualified white applicants." In the bare majority's view, the pertinent provision of the 1866 law simply prohibited private schools from barring students solely because of their race. The two schools now took their case to the U.S. Supreme Court, where the U.S. Department of Justice submitted a brief *amicus curiae* on the side of the black applicants. The Court's answer came quickly in an historic 7:2 (5:2:2) decision.[321] Written by Mr. Justice Stewart, who was joined by his colleagues Burger, Brennan, Marshall, and Blackmun—Justices Powell and Stevens concurring separately and with considerable misgiving[322]—the Supreme Court upheld the lower courts, ruling that "private, commercially operated, non-sectarian schools" may not deny "admission to prospective students because they are Negroes." Over a strongly worded dissenting opinion by Mr. Justice White, who was joined by Mr. Justice Rehnquist, the Court majority based its ruling on the aforementioned section (§1981) of the Civil Rights Acts of 1966—passed to enforce the Thirteenth Amendment's ban on slavery—that accords "all persons

[318] *McCrary v. Runyon,* 363 F. Supp. 1200 (1973).

[319] See my *Justices and Presidents: A Political History of Appointments to the Supreme Court* (New York: Oxford University Press, 1974 and Penguin Press, 1975), especially Chapter I.

[320] *McCrary v. Runyon,* 515 F. 2d 1052 (1975).

[321] *Runyon v. McCrary,* 427 U.S. 160 (1976).

[322] *Ibid.,* at 186, 189. Their reluctant concurrences came almost solely because of what they viewed as the binding 1968 precedent of the *Mayer* decision (footnote 303, p. 384, *supra*), also citing the *"mores* of the day." Powell admitted that he would have sided with the dissenters "if the slate were clean," and Stevens, while acknowledging an almost certain misinterpretation of the Act of 1866 by the majority, pointed to the Court's need for and "interest in stability in orderly development of the law."

the same rights to make and enforce contracts as is enjoyed by white citizens." In response to the schools' contention that this interpretation and application of the statute violate constitutional guarantees of freedom of association, the right to privacy, and parental rights, the controlling opinion found no invasions of any of these safeguards, holding that they "do not provide easy or ready escapes" through which whites "can contravene laws enacted by Congress to enforce the Constitutional right to equality."

But Mr. Justice White viewed the legislative history and intent of the section of the 1866 statute at issue utterly differently than did the five-member majority. It confirms, he wrote in his dissenting opinion,

> that the statute means what it says and no more, *i.e.*, that it outlaws any legal rule disabling any person from making or enforcing a contract, but does not prohibit private racial motivated refusals to contract. . . . What is conferred by [the disputed section of the law] is the right—which was enjoyed by whites—"to make contracts with other willing parties and to enforce those contracts in court." . . . The statute by its terms does not *require* any *private* individual or institution to enter into a contract or perform any other act under any circumstances, and it consequently fails to supply a cause of action by respondent students against petitioned schools based on the latter's racially motivated decision not to contract with them.[323]

In language and philosophy reminiscent of Justices Harlan, II, and Frankfurter, he concluded by flaying his colleagues for undertaking the political task of "construing a statute. . . . a task appropriate for the legislature, not the judiciary."

Left intriguingly unanswered until a future day and Court by Justice Stewart's majority opinion, were such tantalizing questions as the right of *sectarian* schools to discriminate on the basis of race and, conceivably, the application of the 1866 statute to *private clubs*. What is not difficult to predict is that there will be future litigation involving that fascinatingly vexatious line between liberty and equality!

Thus we return to the basic question of establishing a viable line between "private" and "state" action. Does the line *really* serve the desired purpose when it is applied to such utterly routine governmental services as business registration, licensing,[324] contract enforcement, or probation of wills? One may question the choice of the adjective "utterly" in conjunction with "routine services" yet still acknowledge that when services such as those indicated are categorized as "state action" the private sector becomes an anomaly. Perhaps this has happened, but it is doubtful that a majority of the

[323] *Ibid.*, at 195–95.

[324] See *Jackson v. Metropolitan Edison Co.*, 419 U.S. 345 (1974), in which the Court, dividing 6:3, held that a Pennsylvania electric company was not related closely enough to the state government merely because it held a license to service, and that consumers were hence unable to raise "due process of law" claims.

American polity would subscribe to such a conclusion. In Mr. Justice Harlan's observation, "[t]he times have changed [but] perhaps it is appropriate to observe that . . . the equal protection clause of [the Fourteenth] Amendment [does not] rigidly impose upon America an ideology of unrestrained egalitarianism."[325] For, as he had commented on an earlier occasion: "Freedom of the individual to choose his associates or his neighbors, to use and dispose of his property as he sees fit, to be irrational, arbitrary, capricious, even unjust in his personal relations, are things all entitled to a large measure of protection from governmental interference."[326] And as Professor Joseph Tussman, a proved and dedicated partisan of the cause of civil rights and liberties, put the matter of the private-public distinction:

> Do we really want, in the end, to make impossible an Armenian or Jewish Home for the Aged? Do we really wish to deny to the harassed ethnocentric commuter to the polyglot city the solace of spending the evenings of his life in the bosom of a monochromatic suburb? Must the Black Muslims admit White Christians? Must the Far Eastern Cafe hire blond waiters? Cannot the Cosmos Club be silly without losing its liquor license? Is there not some point of saying that much must wait on the slow process of education and maturation?[327]

One can wholly support, encourage, fight for, and even die for, the eradication of the fundamental injustices in the realm of racial discrimination: Equality before the law and of economic, educational, and cultural opportunity; the suffrage; access to the rewards and responsibilities of public office; the end of state-supported or state-permitted or state-enforced segregation—these are the aspects of the problem that should, and do matter! In contrast, those marginal areas of wills and clubs and societies seem unimportant. There *is* something to be said for privacy of association, no matter how silly, undemocratic, or puerile. While, generally, the "equal protection" clause does preclude state enforcement of private discrimination, there may thus well be, in the words of Professor Louis Henkin, one of the foremost students of the field—and a devoted libertarian—"a small area of liberty favored by the Constitution even over claims to equality. Rights of liberty and property, of privacy and voluntary association, must be balanced, in close cases, against the right not to have the state enforce discrimination against the victim. In the few instances in which the right to discriminate is protected or preferred by the Constitution, the state may enforce it."[328]

---

[325] *Harper v. Virginia Board of Elections,* 383 U.S. 663 (1965), dissenting opinion, at 678.

[326] *Lombard v. Louisiana,* 373 U.S. 267 (1963), dissenting opinion, at 250.

[327] Ed., *The Supreme Court on Racial Discrimination* (New York: Oxford University Press, 1963), p. 5. Reprinted by permission.

[328] *"Shelley v. Kraemer,* Notes for a Revised Opinion," *op. cit.,* p. 496.

Unquestionably, this stance raises as many problems as it professes to solve, but a dogmatic approach is no answer either. In part, of course, such legislation as the public accommodations title of the Civil Rights Act of 1964, enacted by the nation's legislative representatives, and subsequently upheld by the Supreme Court, settles the matter in an orderly and legal fashion. So does the "open housing" section of the Civil Rights Act of 1968—whatever one's view of its wisdom.

Yet not all aspects of the vexatious public versus private problem can be conclusively settled by legislative action, nor should they be. There will always be gray areas that should be treated with common sense—a common sense cognizant of our responsibilities as well as our ideals, a common sense that is conscious both of constitutional commands and of the need to strike a balance between liberty and equality. When all other avenues fail, the last word will have to be given by the judiciary, that branch of our government that has proved itself more capable than any other of guarding our basic civil rights and liberties. As Mr. Justice Douglas once wrote: "The people should know that when filibusters occupy other forums, when oppressions are great, when the clash of authority between the individual and the State is severe, they can still get justice in the courts."[329]

Gender-Based Discrimination

In a host of ways, although superficially differing in kind, degree, and genesis, discrimination on the basis of sex—or, perhaps more appropriately termed, gender-based discrimination—is part and parcel of the past American dilemma. Gender-based discrimination is now largely a practice that is constitutionally impermissible. Although there has long been a "women's movement," the issue of invidious discrimination in the realm of gender did not really impress itself upon the public conscience until the desegregation movement evolved close to its crescendo in the 1960s. And, as has been so true of racial discrimination, it would again be the judiciary that was called upon to articulate and to mandate egalitarianism and equal opportunity in the realm of sex, based upon the implicit and explicit commands of the "equal protection of the laws" and the "due process of law" clauses of the basic document.

A difference in the Supreme Court's approach to the problem, however, has surfaced in its unwillingness to date (Summer 1981) to accord "suspect" category status to gender-based legislative classifications. Although four Justices have evinced a desire to place sex on the same footing as race, and thus to consider both on the "suspect" plane, a clear majority has so

---

[329] *Bell v. Maryland,* 378 U.S. 226 (1964), concurring opinion, at 242–45.

far preferred "close" or "very close" scrutiny. It is conceivable that the adoption of the Equal Rights Amendment (ERA) would naturally compel a change in the judicial attitude, but that remains to be seen. Meanwhile—as the numerous references to court cases in the gender-based sector of public law throughout the foregone pages have indicated—the Court has followed an approach that appears to vary between the "rationality" test for legislation (e.g., see *Reed v. Reed,* in Table 7.1) and that of a "compelling state interest" (e.g., see *Frontiero v. Richardson*). In *both* instances the allegations by women of invidious gender-based discrimination prevailed, unanimously in the first and 8:1 in the second case.

As the accompanying table on gender-based discrimination decisions readily indicates, there remains little doubt that—as has also been demonstrably true of the realm of racial discrimination—great strides, judicially punctuated and confirmed, have been made along the road toward the eradication not only of invidious discrimination but also of the arguably non-invidious kind. The latter category is personified by some of the actions taken and decisions rendered as a result of congressional enactment of what became generally known as "Title IX." That visible section of the Education Amendments of 1972 bars, with certain exceptions, discrimination on the basis of sex in any education program receiving federal assistance. The resultant welter of regulations issued by the Department of Health, Education, and Welfare did much to remedy past wrongs; but it also did much to drive coaches of the so-called "contact" sports, especially of the revenue-producing kind, up the proverbial wall. They appear to have survived, however.

The controversial enactment of the draft-registration statute of 1980, which specifically *excluded* women, created predictable controversy by friend and foe of sexual equality alike, all of which tended to blur lines between otherwise predictable supporters and opponents of legislative classification by gender. A major class-action suit was filed almost instantly in federal court by a group of *male* registrants, alleging invidious sex discrimination. *Either,* so the argument goes, the exclusion of women constitutes a violation of *their* Fifth Amendment constitutional rights of due process of law ("equal protection" *per se* not being applicable because it is confined to *state* infractions under the Fourteenth Amendment), *or* it constitutes a violation of the rights of *males* because they are being "singled out." The Court's answer came in June 1981 (*Rostker v. Goldberg,* 49 LW 4798). It ruled 6:3 that the registration provisions excluding women do not violate the Fifth Amendment; that Congress acted well within its constitutional authority to raise and regulate armies and navies, noting that the "customary deference" according Congress's judgments is "particularly appropriate" in national defense and military affairs.

Table 7.1

REPRESENTATIVE DECISIONS BY THE UNITED STATES SUPREME COURT IN
RECENT GENDER-BASED DISCRIMINATION CASES

CASE	YEAR DECIDED	ISSUE AND DISPOSITION	VOTE	DISSENTS
Reed v. Reed, 404 U.S. 71	1971	State of Idaho gave preference to made in intestate administration. Declared a violation of the equal protection clause of the Fourteenth Amendment.	9:0	None
Frontiero v. Richardson, 411 U.S. 677	1973	Federal law that automatically qualified male service personnel for spousal benefits but that required female personnel to show proof of dependency. Declared unconstitutional infringement of due process clause of the Fifth Amendment.	8:1	Rehnquist
Kahn v. Shevin, 416 U.S. 351	1974	Florida law granting widows but not widowers $500 property-tax exemption. Declared constitutional because a woman's loss of spouse imposed greater financial disability usually than a man's loss of spouse.	6:3	Douglas Brennan Marshall
Geduldig v. Aiello, 417 U.S. 484	1974	State of California disability insurance payments to private employees not covered by workmen's compensation, *excluding* normal pregnancies, among other disabilities. Upheld as a rational choice by state.	6:3	Douglas Brennan Marshall
Schlesinger v. Ballard, 419 U.S. 498	1975	Federal law on mandatory Navy discharges: women guaranteed 13 years of service; men automatically discharged after failing twice to be promoted. Upheld as rational because women have less opportunity for promotion.	5:4	Douglas Brennan Marshall White
Taylor v. Louisiana, 419 U.S. 522	1975	Louisiana statutory and constitutional provisions excluding women from juries unless they manifest a desire to serve via a written request. Declared unconstitutional as violation of equal protection clause of the Fourteenth Amendment.	8:1	Rehnquist
Stanton v. Stanton, 421 U.S. 7	1975	Utah law that provides for lower age of majority for girls than for boys in connection with parental obligation to pay child support. Struck down as irrational.	8:1	Rehnquist

Case	Year	Description	Vote	Justices
General Electric Co. v. Gilbert, 429 U.S. 125	1976	Private employer's disability plan excluded pregnancies from coverage. Upheld as not invidiously discriminatory under due process of law clause of the Fifth Amendment.	6:3	Brennan Marshall Stevens
Craig v. Boren, 429 U.S. 190	1976	Oklahoma statute prohibiting sale of 3.2 per cent beer to males under 21 years of age but to females only under 18. Held to be invidiously discriminatory under equal protection clause of the Fourteenth Amendment.	7:2	Burger Rehnquist
Califano v. Webster, 430 U.S. 313	1977	Section of federal Social Security Act providing that wives may exclude three more of their lower earning years in computing average wage for retirement benefits than husbands may. Upheld as "benign," not illogical, and thus not constitutionally defective.	9:0	None
City of Los Angeles Department of Water v. Manhart, 435 U.S. 702	1978	Municipal regulation that required female employees to pay 15 per cent more into pension fund than male employees because women expect statistically to live longer than men. Declared unconstitutional as violation of equal protection of the laws clause of Amendment Fourteen.	6:2	Burger Rehnquist
Orr v. Orr, 440 U.S. 268	1979	Alabama law providing that husbands but not wives are liable to pay post-divorce alimony. Struck down as violation of equal protection clause of Fourteenth Amendment.	6:3	Burger Powell Rehnquist
Califano v. Westcott, 443 U.S. 76	1979	Section of federal Social Security Act providing benefits to needy dependent children only because of father's unemployment, not because of mother's. Struck down as violation of the due process clause of the Fifth Amendment.	9:0	None
Wengler v. Druggists Mutual Insurance Co., 100 S.Ct. 1540	1980	Section of Missouri's workmen's compensation law that requires a husband to prove actual dependence on his spouse's earnings but does not require wife to prove such dependence. Declared unconstitutional as violation of the equal protection clause of the Fourteenth Amendment.	8:1	Rehnquist
Michael M. v. Superior Court, 49 LW 4273	1981	California statutory rape law punishing males, but not females, for sexual intercourse with an underage partner of the opposite sex upheld as not irrational because "only women may become pregnant."	5:4	Brennan White Marshall Stevens

The Wrench of "Reverse Discrimination"

As the history of the post-World War II period, especially the post-Brown I and II[330] days—and, it is hoped, the pages of this chapter—have demonstrated incontestably, the advances on the desegregation-integration front have been as widespread and evident as they have been gratifying. The nation, led by the judiciary, then joined by the executive and legislative branches, acknowledged the injustices of the past and proceeded, however gradually at first, to make amends.

Yet much remains to be done, in particular on the economic front. It is thus hardly surprising that the 1960s and, more insistently, the 1970s have brought demands from blacks, as well as other minority groups and, of course, women, that programs be established, both in and out of government, that will go well beyond "mere" equality of opportunity and provide compensatory treatment for the injustices of two centuries by commitments not only to remedial action but to outright preferment on a host of fronts, headed by employment and education. Known as "affirmative action" to bring about increased minority employment opportunities, promotions, and admissions to colleges and universities, among others, the programs soon became controversial because of their use of *quotas,* also euphemistically called "goals" and/or "guidelines." In other words, the basic plea, along with the philosophy of the *proponents* of "affirmative action," was (and is) that it is not enough to provide a full measure of absolute equality of opportunity, based upon individual merit. Given the ravages of the past, preferential treatment must be accorded through affirmative action that all but guarantees numerically, in effect, targeted slots or posts based upon membership in racial (and sexual) groups. The *opponents* of such a course of public, and, to a lesser degree, private policy do not necessarily object to affirmative action *per se*—such as aggressive recruiting, remedial training (no matter what the expense), and perhaps even what Mr. Justice Powell in the *Bakke* case styled a "plus" consideration of race along with other equitable factors.[331] But they do object to policies that may be regarded as "reverse discrimination," generally comprising such as the *numerus clausus* (rigid quotas set aside to benefit identifiable racial or other groups), as in the *Weber* case;[332] double standards in grading, rating, ranking, and similar requirements on the employment, educational, and other pertinent fronts of opportunity; and so-called "set aside" laws that guarantee specified percentages of contracts to minority groups, as in the *Fullilove* case.[333]

---

[330] *Brown v. Board of Education of Topeka,* 347 U.S. 483 (1954) and 349 U.S. 294 (1955)—commonly referred to as *"Brown I"* and *"Brown II,"* respectively.
[331] *Regents of the University of California v. Bakke,* 438 U.S. 265 (1978), at 317.
[332] *United Steelworkers of America v. Weber,* 443 U.S. 193 (1979).
[333] *Fullilove v. Klutznick,* 48 LW 4979 (1980).

The Bakke Case. It was a foregone conclusion that, sooner or later, the "reverse discrimination" issue(s) would reach the Supreme Court—especially in view of what seems to be the proscriptive intent of the Fourteenth Amendment with respect to race; judicial precedents pointing to "color blindness"; and, perhaps most clearly, the ringing mandates of both the language and the intent of the seminal Civil Rights Act of 1964, in general, and Titles VI and VII, in particular.[334] As described earlier, the high tribunal was far from eager to come to grips with this explosive, emotion-charged, delicate, and vexatious issue, and it had managed to moot it in its non-decision *De Funis* decision of 1964.[335] But events would not be denied, and the nine Justices confronted on its merits—more or less—the "reverse discrimination" aspect of "affirmative action" for the first time in the now historic *Bakke* case of 1978. Yet the long-in-coming ruling provided neither clearcut "winners" nor clearcut "losers"—and that may well be precisely what the Justices intended. Still, disappointment by friends, foes, and neutrals was widespread; for very little was in fact finally settled by *Bakke.* The verbose opinions that were handed down were seriously divided—a stark contrast to the brief, unanimous decision in the seminal *Brown I and II* cases[336] a quarter of a century earlier. Still, the multiple six-opinion, 154-page judgments did spell out some basics, although the case neither settled, nor did it pretend to settle, the ongoing controversy at issue.

Essentially, and summarily, three identifiable groups of Justices rendered at least three different opinions; the two controlling ones were fashioned by the swing vote of the key Justice in the case, Lewis F. Powell, Jr. In one of these, joined by Justices Stevens, Stewart, Rehnquist, and Chief Justice Burger, Powell's 5:4 stewardship affirmed the California judiciary's decision ordering the University of California's Medical School at Davis to admit Allan Bakke, a white applicant, who had twice been rejected by Davis, notwithstanding the University-stipulated fact that he was more highly qualified than any of the admittees from the sixteen-member minority group. These students had entered the Medical School under a special program that had set aside, on an *admitted* quota basis, sixteen of the hundred openings at the school for "minorities." Justice Powell held the University's action to be an unconstitutional violation of the equal protection of the laws clause of the Fourteenth Amendment, whereas the other four regarded *any* racial quota systems utilized by government-supported programs (such as higher education) to be an obvious violation of the explicit language of Title VI of the Civil Rights Act of 1964. The four dissenters, Justices Brennan, White, Marshall, and Blackmun, on the other hand, saw

[334] See pp. 348–50, *supra,* for the Act's main titles and commentary.
[335] See p. 323, footnote 58, and p. 349, footnote 161, *supra.*
[336] See p. 396, footnote 330, *supra.*

neither a constitutional nor a statutory infraction; they called for the per-
missive use of race as a justifiable "compensatory" action to redress past
wrongs generally. (No racial discrimination against blacks or any other
minorities had ever been charged against the University of California at
Davis.) While refusing to join these four in so expansive a constitutional
stance, Justice Powell nevertheless also held for them and himself (5:4)
that the California courts had been wrong in ruling that race could *never*
be a factor in admissions decisions (the state's judiciary had been *adjudg-
ing* such a practice to be *both* illegal *and* unconstitutional); that a state
university had "a substantial interest" in a diverse student body "that le-
gitimately may be served [here pointing to Harvard] by a properly devised
admission program involving the competitive consideration of race and
ethnic origin."[337]

What the Supreme Court did, then, in *Bakke* was: (1) to disallow (5:4)
the kind of explicit, specific, rigid racial quota established by California;
and (2) to uphold (5:4) the use of "race" as a tool of affirmative action
programs in the absence of Davis-like quota arrangements; but—at least
for the time being—(3) to reject (4:5) the interpretation by the Stevens,
Stewart, Rehnquist, Burger group that found the use of race in *any* programs benefitting from federal financial assistance to be illegal; and also
(4) to reject (4:5), at least by implication, the position of the Brennan,
White, Marshall, Blackmun group that the "affirmative action" use of race,
far from being constitutionally proscribed, was permitted. In a sense, then,
the *Wall Street Journal* was justified in headlining the *Bakke* verdict as
"The Decision Everyone Won"[338]—although, *de minimis,* that statement
needs both considerable explication and qualification. In fine, the Court's
long-awaited decision left intact the bulk of affirmative action programs
that give special consideration to statutorily identified minority groups
(and women), while running up a *caveat* flag on obvious, *rigid* racial (and,
by implication, probably sexual and other) quotas. The controversial matter at issue in *Bakke*—confined, as it was, to higher education—hardly settled the overall "reverse discrimination" problem. In 1979 a string of cases,
winding its way through the judicial structure toward the highest court of
the land, was headed by a number of potentially seminal "quota cases" in
education[339] and, particularly and naturally, in employment.

Weber. Among the cases in the "judicial mill" was the *Weber* case,[340]
decided by the Supreme Court one year after *Bakke.* Together with the lat-

[337] *Bakke, op. cit.,* at 321–24.
[338] June 29, 1978, p. 1.
[339] By the margin of one vote the Court declined in 1979 to review the case of an
Italian-American New Yorker whose application under the University of Colorado
Law School's special admissions program for blacks, Chicanos, and American Indians
had been refused consideration because he did not "belong" to any of the eligible
groups. (*DiLeo v. Board of Regents,* 441 U.S. 927.)
[340] *United Steelworkers of America v. Weber,* 443 U.S. 193 (1979).

ter and the forthcoming 1980 *Fullilove* decision,[341] it would become one of the triad of "reverse discrimination" cases that, in effect, provided a green light or at least a green-and-yellow one, for the widespread affirmative action programs pushed aggressively by the Carter Administration.

At issue in *Weber* was an allegedly "voluntary" and "temporary" affirmative action plan devised by the Kaiser Aluminum and Chemical Corporation and the United Steelworkers of America for Kaiser's Gramercy, Louisiana, plant, under which at least one-half of the available thirteen positions in an on-the-job training program had been reserved for blacks. Finding himself excluded solely because he was white, Brian Weber filed suit in federal district court, claiming a *prima facie* violation of Title VII of the Civil Rights Act of 1964, which categorically bans any racial discrimination in employment, no matter whether the individual's race be black, white (or any other color), and which specifically states that its provisions are not to be interpreted "to require any employer . . . to grant preferential treatment to any individual or to any group because of the race . . . of such individual or group." Moreover, the congressional history of the statute's enactment made crystal clear that Congress meant precisely what it said, and that the Civil Rights Act's proponents had so assured the doubters during the exciting eighty-three days of floor debate in 1964.[342] Basing their decisions on *both* the language of Title VII and that of the congressional debates, enshrined in the *Congressional Record,* the two lower federal courts that had ajudicated the case[343] upheld Weber's contentions and ruled the affirmative action plan at issue to be illegal under Title VII.

But in an astonishing decision, handed down during the last week of its 1978–79 term, the Supreme Court reversed the courts below in a 5:2 holding, Justices Powell and Stevens abstaining. Writing for the majority, Mr. Justice Brennan (joined by Justices Marshall, Stewart, and White and, with reservations, by Justice Blackmun) frankly conceded that the rulings by the lower courts had *followed the letter* of the Civil Rights Act of 1964 but not its *spirit.* He conjectured that Congress's primary concern had been with "the plight of the Negro in our economy," and that it would be "ironic indeed" if Title VII would be used to prohibit "all voluntary private, race-conscious efforts to abolish traditional patterns" of discrimination.[344]

Mr. Chief Justice Burger and Mr. Justice Rehnquist dissented vehe-

---

[341] *Fullilove v. Klutznick,* 48 LW 4979 (1980).

[342] Thus, an exchange between the C.R.A.'s floor manager, Senator Hubert H. Humphrey (D.–Minn.) and a principal opponent, Senator Willis Robertson (D.–Va.): "If the Senator can find in Title VII . . . any language which provides that an employer will have to hire on the basis of percentage or quota related to color . . . I will start eating the pages, one after another, because it is not in there." (110 Cong. Rec. 7420.)

[343] 415 F. Supp. 761 and 563 F. 2d 216 (1977).

[344] *Weber, op. cit.,* at 201.

mently, charging that the majority had engaged in the crassest kind of judicial activism, which amounted to blatant judicial legislation; that it had, in fact, "totally rewritten a crucial part" of the law. As a member of Congress, the Chief Justice admonished, he "would be inclined to vote for" the views expressed by the majority; but as a judge he had no business in writing legislation. "Congress," he explained with feeling, "expressly *prohibited* the discrimination against Brian Weber" that the five-member majority now approved.[345] And in what may well constitute one of the angriest dissenting opinions in recent times, Justice Rehnquist accused the Court majority of acting like Harry Houdini, the escape artist.[346] Congress sought to require racial equality in government, Rehnquist contended, and "there is perhaps no device more destructive to the notion of equality than . . . the quota. Whether described as 'benign discrimination' or 'affirmative action,' the racial quota is nonetheless a creator of castes, a two-edged sword that must demean one in order to prefer the other." He concluded:

> With today's holding, the Court introduces . . . a tolerance for the very evil that the law was intended to eradicate, without offering even a clue as to what the limits on that tolerance may be. . . . The Court has sown the wind. Later courts will face the impossible task of reaping the whirlwind.[347]

Fullilove. Since the *Weber* majority held that, notwithstanding prohibitory statutory language, racial quotas were neither illegal nor unconstitutional if adopted on a "voluntary" and "temporary" basis, the Court's six-opinion "reverse-discrimination" decision in *Fullilove v. Klutznick*[348] one year later did not come as a major surprise. For, at issue in the latter case was the constitutionality of a 1977 congressional law that, in a floor amendment, adopted without prior hearings, had set aside 10 per cent of a $4 billion public works program for "minority business enterprises," defined in the statute as companies in which blacks, Hispanic-Americans, Oriental-Americans, American Indians, Eskimos, or Aleuts controlled at least a 50 per cent interest. What was surprising was that the governing plurality opinion was written by the Chief Justice, who had so sternly dissented in *Weber*.[349] But speaking also for Justices White and Powell—with the latter also filing a separate concurring opinion,[350]—and joined on far more expansively permissive grounds in another concurrence by Mr. Justice Marshall, who in turn was joined by Justices Brennan and Blackmun[351]—Mr. Chief Justice Burger found warrant for his ruling that the pro-

---

[345] *Ibid.,* at 218. (Italics in original.)
[346] *Ibid.,* at 222.
[347] *Ibid.,* at 255.
[348] 48 LW 4979 (1980).
[349] *United Steelworkers of America v. Weber,* 443 U.S. 193 (1979).
[350] *Fullilove v. Klutznick, op. cit.,* at 4992.
[351] *Ibid.,* at 4998.

gram did "not violate the equal protection component of the Due Process Clause of the Fifth Amendment"[352] in the power of Congress "to enforce by appropriate legislation" the equal protection guarantees of the Fourteenth Amendment.[353] Rejecting the contention by the non-minority business enterprises that Congress is obligated to act in a "color blind" fashion, and is in fact forbidden to employ racial quotas under the Constitution's mandates, he referred repeatedly to what he viewed as the temporary nature of the "narrowly tailored" program, one designed by the national legislature to remedy long-standing past wrongs.[354]

There were three vocal dissenters, their leading opinion being written by Mr. Justice Stewart, who had joined the majority in *Weber* but had been on the other side in *Bakke*. This dissenting opinion was also signed by Mr. Justice Rehnquist, who consistently opposed racial quotas in all three cases. The other dissent was filed by Mr. Justice Stevens, who did not sit in *Weber,* but whose views were in accord with Rehnquist in *Bakke* as well as now in *Fullilove*. Bristling with anger, Stewart accused his colleagues on the other side of the decision of having rendered a "racist" decision[355] an adjective he veritably spit out while reading his dissent in full from the bench on that 1980 July Opinion Day. Styling the "set-aside law" an "invidious discrimination by government," he pleaded that the Constitution permits no discrimination of any kind between the races; that the

> Fourteenth Amendment was adopted to ensure that every person must be treated equally by each State regardless of the color of his skin . . . that it would honor no preference based on lineage . . .[356]

and he concluded:

> Today the Court derails this achievement and places its imprimatur on the creation once again by government of privileges based on birth.[357]

In his even more scathing dissenting opinion, which he read aloud from the bench on the day of the decision, Mr. Justice Stevens charged that the "minority set-aside law" represents a "perverse form of reparation," a "slapdash" law that rewards some who may not need rewarding and hurts others who may not deserve hurting.[358] Suggesting that such a law could be used simply as a patronage tool by its authors, he warned that it could

[352] *Ibid.,* at 4980.
[353] *Ibid.,* at 4987.
[354] *Ibid.,* at 4990.
[355] *Ibid.,* at 5002.
[356] *Ibid.,* at 5006.
[358] *Ibid.,* at 5003–04.
[357] *Ibid.,* at 5002.

breed more resentment and prejudice than it corrects,[359] and he asked what percentage of "oriental blood or what degree of Spanish-speaking skill is required for membership in the preferred class?"[360] Sarcastically, he said that now the government must devise its version of the Nazi laws that defined who is a Jew, musing that "our statute books will once again have to contain laws that reflect the odious practice of delineating the qualities that make one person a Negro and make another white."[361]

Coda

The *Bakke, Weber,* and *Fullilove* rulings once again underscore not only the wrench of the quest for equal justice under law but also the omnipresent question of the judicial role—of how to draw that line between judicial restraint and judicial activism, between the judiciary's presumed role of finding rather than making the law and its other assumed role of being the country's "conscience."[362] As for the issue of "reverse discrimination"— with several new cases on the Court's 1980–81 docket which again promise renewed controversy—the words of Philip B. Kurland, one of the country's foremost experts on constitutional law and history, are worth keeping in mind. In his view the entire syndrome will almost certainly be with us for years to come, given what he regards as the "fundamental shift of constitutional limitations from protection of individual rights to protection of class rights . . . to the measurement of equality of opportunity to equality of condition or result."[363]

To the Supreme Court of the United States we have thus turned again and again to help us in our unending need to draw lines. Despite the storms of controversy that have engulfed it, it has remained true to its acquired role as our national conscience and our institutional common sense. In the long run, if not always in the short, the Court has served us well in maintaining that blend of change and continuity that is so necessary to the stability of the governmental process of a democracy. It has seemed to adhere to the basic American value so beautifully phrased by Thomas Jefferson and inscribed around the ceiling of the rotunda of the Jefferson Memorial: "I have sworn upon the altar of God eternal hostility against every form of tyranny over the mind of man."

---

[359] *Ibid.,* at 5005.

[360] *Ibid.,* at 5007.

[361] *Ibid.,* at 5002–03. Cf. the Court's 1981 *disallowance* of a 25% set-aside California construction quota program (101 S. Ct. 783).

[362] See my *The Judicial Process* . . . , 4th ed. (New York: Oxford University Press, 1980), Chapters VII, VIII, and IX.

[363] "The Private I . . . ," X, *The University of Chicago Record* 4 (July 19, 1976).

Bibliographical Note

The nature of the relationship of the judicial process to civil rights and liberties has been the subject of a profusion of pertinent writings. In the first edition of my *The Judicial Process: An Introductory Analysis of the Courts of the United States, England, and France* (Oxford University Press, 1962), I compiled four separate bibliographies of constitutional law totaling some twelve hundred books. The fourth, which appeared in 1980, featured some 4,500 entries; not all of these apply here, of course, but a good many do so, at least tangentially. Yet specific works on the problem of "line-drawing" itself are scarce indeed; most of the published material treats the problem implicitly, rather than explicitly, and within the context of the particular publication's theme. On the other hand, there are some trenchant and stimulating works, generally relatively brief and topical, that do address themselves to line-drawing in a few selected fields. Among these are Sidney Hook's thoughtful *The Paradoxes of Freedom* (University of California Press, 1962), which deals with "intelligence and human rights," "democracy and judicial review," and "intelligence, conscience, and the right to revolution"; David Fellman's *The Limits of Freedom* (Rutgers University Press, 1959), an incisive consideration of religious freedom, "the right to communicate," and "the right to talk politics"; Arthur M. Okun's intriguing study, *Equality and Efficiency: The Big Tradeoff* (Brookings, 1975), in which he analyzes the timely aspect of current line-drawing with insight and perception; and J. M. Buchanan's *Between Anarchy and Leviathan: The Limits of Liberty* (University of Chicago Press, 1975), which deals engagingly with the rule of law, the judicial process, and certain rights of the citizen in democratic society. Milton R. Konvitz's *Expanding Liberties* enjoys a telling designated subtitle, "The Emergence of New Civil Liberties and Civil Rights in Postwar America" (Viking, 1967). The reader, *New Dimensions of Freedom in America* (Chandler, 1969), ably edited by Frederick M. Wirt and Willis D. Hawley, is a useful compendium of "position" essays. And there is the magnificent little gem by that great American, Mr. Justice Hugo LaFayette Black, *A Constitutional Faith* (Alfred A. Knopf, 1968), which shines with first principles.

The "double standard," discussed in my second chapter, has absorbed and troubled many students of the judicial process: Paul A. Freund outlines its difficulties in his *The Supreme Court of the United States: Its Business and*

Purposes (Meridian Press, 1961); Judge Learned Hand opposes it in—among other works—*The Bill of Rights* (Harvard University Press, 1958); Mr. Justice Hugo L. Black upholds it in many of his opinions and, most dramatically perhaps, in his famous essay "The Bill of Rights," 35 *New York University Law Review* 866 (April 1960); Loren P. Beth favors it in "The Case for Judicial Protection of Civil Liberties," 17 *The Journal of Politics* 112 (February 1955); Robert G. McCloskey is critical of it in "Economic Due Process and the Supreme Court: An Exhumation and Reburial," in Philip B. Kurland, ed., *The Supreme Court Review* 1962 (University of Chicago Press, 1962), pp. 34–62; and so is Bernard H. Siegan in his *Economic Liberties and The Constitution* (University of Chicago Press, 1980). An exchange between Richard Funston and me on the justifiability of its existence appeared in 90 *Political Science Quarterly* 2 (Summer 1975). Important analyses and evaluations of the "new" double standard, linked to the "new" or "substantive" equal protection *cum* "suspect categories" approach to the problem are, among many others: Gerald Gunther, "The Supreme Court: 1971 Term; In Search of Evolving Doctrine on a Changing Court: A Model for a Newer Equal Protection," 86 *Harvard Law Review* 1 (1972); J. Harvie Wilkinson, III, "The Supreme Court, the Equal Protection Clause, and the Three Faces of Constitutional Equality," 61 *Virginia Law Review* 945 (1975); and Robert G. Dixon, Jr., "The 'New' Substantive Due Process and the Democratic Ethic: A Prolegomenon," 1 *Brigham Young Law Review* 1 (1976). A good historical "period" work is Arnold M. Paul, *Conservative Crisis and the Rule of Law, 1889–1895*, rev. ed. (Harper & Row, 1969).

Further reading on "The Bill of Rights and Its Applicability to the States," the topic of Chapter III, may be done in a number of works. Robert A. Rutland's *The Birth of the Bill of Rights, 1776–1791* (Collier Books, 1962), provides valuable background to the document's purpose and framing. The elusive intentions of the framers of the Fourteenth Amendment, which have been interpreted and reinterpreted from all points of view often with diametrically opposed conclusions, should not be considered without some reference to the records of the actual debates in the 39th Congress during 1866. *The Globe* will help. The major protagonists in the controversy over "incorporation" of the Bill of Rights are identified and evaluated both in the text and in the footnotes in Chapter III, especially between pages 40 and 57, so that there is no need to cite them here. While there is very little material available on the evolution of "incorporation" or "absorption" and the position of the justices, a host of writings, chiefly journal articles, exist on specific clauses of the Bill of Rights and on the attitudes of the justices. A perusal of the *Index to Legal Periodicals*, the *Public Affairs Information Service*, and the *Reader's Guide to Periodical Literature* will provide a good many citations. The leading Supreme Court decisions themselves are rich natural fare for analysis and debate. Thus, *Palko v. Connecticut*, 302 U.S. 319 (1937), *Adamson v. California*, 332 U.S. 46 (1947); *Griswold v. Connecticut*, 381 U.S. 479 (1965); and *Duncan v. Louisiana*, 391 U.S. 145 (1968), to name just four, feature numerous opinions on the question of applying the Bill of Rights to several states of the Union. A good summary of its evolution is available in Arthur A. North, S.J., *The Su-*

preme Court: Judicial Process and Judicial Politics (Appleton-Century-Crofts, 1966). Mr. Justice Black's essay, "The Bill of Rights," and his *A Constitutional Faith* are again pertinent here; and a sophisticated analysis of the position is presented by Norman G. Rudman in "Incorporation Under the Fourteenth Amendment—The Other Side of the Coin," in 3 *Law in Transition Quarterly* 3 (Spring 1966). An excellent full-length study is Richard C. Cortner's *The Supreme Court and the Second Bill of Rights* (University of Wisconsin Press, 1981).

"Due process" and questions of criminal justice are ever timely and are treated in many media. The Supreme Court's "liberalizing" decisions in this field, beginning about 1961, have given rise to a stream of commentaries in the daily press, the weeklies, and sundry journals. That stream became a flood after the Warren Court's opinions in the landmark cases of *Escobedo v. Illinois*, 378 U.S. 478 (1964), and *Miranda v. Arizona*, 384 U.S. 436 (1966); the end is not in sight. Some fine books on procedural due process generally are David Fellman's *The Defendant's Rights Today* (University of Wisconsin Press, 1976), a superb reference work; Roscoe Pound's still pertinent *Criminal Justice in America* (Holt, 1945); an excellent, fairly recent volume by an active participant in the pursuit of criminal justice, Arnold S. Trebach, *The Rationing of Justice: Constitutional Rights and the Criminal Process* (Rutgers University Press, 1964); and Fred P. Graham's book-length study of the Warren Court's rulings on criminal law, *The Self-Inflicted Wound* (Macmillan, 1970), is a major contribution to the debate. Necessary reading, at least *passim,* are the 1969 and 1970 reports of the National Commission on the Causes and Prevention of Violence (Bantam paperbacks). To cite just a few of the many important books available in specific areas of due process: for two opposite views on the meaning and application of the Fifth Amendment's self-incrimination clause, we have Erwin N. Griswold's *The Fifth Amendment Today* (Harvard University Press, 1955), and Sidney Hook's *Common Sense and the Fifth Amendment* (Criterion Books, 1957); and Leonard W. Levy won a Pulitzer prize for his superb *Origins of the Fifth Amendment* (Oxford University Press, 1968). J. W. Landynski's *Search and Seizure and The Supreme Court* (The Johns Hopkins University Press, 1966), is an important work in constitutional interpretation, and Alan F. Westin tries to find middle ground in the eternally puzzling field of wire-tapping in his *Privacy and Freedom* (Atheneum, 1967); David M. O'Brien's *Privacy, Law, and Public Policy* (Praeger, 1979) deals ably between concepts of privacy and information. There is no better book extant on the right to counsel than Anthony Lewis's justly praised study of the travail of Clarence Earl Gideon, *Gideon's Trumpet* (Random House, 1964); the much neglected problem of bail is persuasively criticized by Ronald Goldfarb in *Ransom* (Harper & Row, 1965); L. G. Miller and J. A. Sigler are on different sides in the continuing controversy on the range of double jeopardy in our federal system in their, respectively, *Double Jeopardy and the Federal System* (University of Chicago Press, 1968) and *Double Jeopardy: The Development of a Legal and Social Policy* (Cornell University Press, 1969); and Judge Marvin E. Frankel makes a thoughtful contribution with his *Criminal Sentences: Law Without Order* (Hill and Wang, 1973). James Q. Wilson, in *Thinking about Crime* (Basic Books, 1975), and Charles Silberman, in *Criminal Violence, Criminal Justice* (Random House, 1978) present masterful, no-nonsense analyses about the nature, causes, prevention, and control of crime; George F. Cole provides a useful reader with his *Criminal Justice: Law and Politics,* 3d ed. (Duxbury, 1980); and Mr. Chief Justice Warren E. Burger's annual "State of the Judiciary" message always contains useful data and exhortations on crime and criminal justice.

There is probably more material available in the area of freedom of expression than in any of the others that I have treated in the book; much of it is mentioned in Chapter V. The classic study is still Zechariah Chafee, Jr., *Free Speech in the United States* (Harvard University Press, 1954); his contributions to the comprehension and appreciation of freedom of expression are towering. The writings, both on and off the bench, of such steadfast supporters of free speech as Justices Holmes, Brandeis, Hughes, Stone, Cardozo, Black, and Douglas deserve the same respect. Other important works are *Free Speech and Its Relation to Self-Government* (Harper, 1948) and *Political Freedom: The Constitutional Powers of the People* (Oxford University Press, 1965) by Alexander Meiklejohn, who taught Chafee but outlived him. Meiklejohn's thesis goes beyond Chafee's limits, but remains a fine testament to freedom of speech and press. Chafee's review of this book in 62 *Harvard Law Review* 891 (1949) is necessary reading for anyone interested in line-drawing on the frontiers of freedom of expression. A timely, if wistful, evaluation of the Meiklejohn position is presented by Mr. Justice William J. Brennan, Jr., in his "The Supreme Court and the Meiklejohn Interpretation of the First Amendment," 79 *Harvard Law Review* 1 (November, 1965). An insightful, albeit questionably successful, endeavor to find and draw that elusive "line" for freedom of expression in relation to proscribable conduct is Thomas I. Emerson's fascinating *Toward a General Theory of the First Amendment* (Vintage, 1967). A long-time student of the free press, John Lofton, has given us a fine treatment of it in his *The Press as Guardian of the First Amendment* (The University of South Carolina Press, 1980), and Charles E. Rice does equally well for association and assembly in *Freedom of Association* (New York University Press, 1962). The nine (!) opinions rendered by the justices in the 1971 *New York Times* and *Washington Post* cases make for a fascinating study of differing approaches to the First Amendment's posture vis-à-vis governmental national security claims. Civil disobedience is examined from varying points of view by such diverse libertarians as Abe Fortas, *Concerning Dissent and Civil Disobedience* (New American Library, 1968); Sidney Hook, *Academic Freedom and Academic Anarchy* (Cowles, 1969); William O. Douglas, *Points of Rebellion* (Random House, 1970); and Howard Zinn, *Disobedience and Democracy* (Random House, 1968). Among important works on the issues of obscenity, morals, and censorship, which are so closely related to freedom of expression, are: Harriet F. Pilpel's *Obscenity and the Constitution* (Bowker, 1973); a superb study by Alexander Meiklejohn's son, Donald, *Freedom and the Public: Public and Private Morality in America* (Syracuse University Press, 1965); an interesting conservative approach by Harry M. Clor, *Obscenity and Public Morality: Censorship in a Liberal Society* (University of Chicago Press, 1969); a concise, realistic monograph by Lane V. Sunderland, *Obscenity: The Court, The Congress and the President's Commission* (American Enterprise Institute, 1974); a controversial behavioral study, *Pornography and Sexual Deviance* (University of California Press, 1974) by Michael J. Goldstein et al.; and an overview of a burgeoning contemporary issue, edited by D. C. Knutson, *Homosexuality and the Law* (Haworth Press, 1980).

There is no dearth of works in the realm of religion, and there is a particularly heavy output on the question of the separation of Church and State. Here Leo Pfeffer's excellent one-volume condensation of Anson Phelps Stokes's monumental *Church and State in the United States* (Harper, 1950), published by Harper and Row in 1964 under the same title, is the key work for both its historical account and its sound analysis—although the author and editor hold controversial points of view. Representative Roman Catholic stances on the matter of separation of Church and State may be found in Robert F. Drinan, *Religion, the Courts, and Public Policy* (McGraw-Hill, 1963); Jerome G. Kerwin, *Catholic Viewpoint on Church and State* (Hanover House, 1959); Neil G. McCluskey, *Catholic Viewpoint on Education* (Hanover House, 1959); and D. M. Kelly, *Why Churches Should Not Pay Taxes* (Harper and Row, 1977). The other side is ardently presented in, for example, Paul Blanshard's *Religion and the Schools: The Great Controversy* (Beacon Press, 1963); Leo Pfeffer's *God, Caesar, and Constitution* (Beacon Press, 1975); and in J. M. Swomley, Jr.'s *Religion, the State and the Schools* (Pegasus, 1969). An excellent collection of diverse viewpoints is *The Wall Between Church and State,* edited by Dallin H. Oaks (University of Chicago, 1963); and a nicely done volume by a political scientist and prominent church layman is Murray S. Stedman's *Religion and Politics in America* (Harcourt, Brace & World, 1964). Among other scholarly works that evaluate the establishment problem ably, are Paul G. Kauper, *Religion and the Constitution* (Louisiana State University Press, 1964); Robert Gordis, *Religion and the Schools* (Fund for the Republic, 1959); R. J. Miller and R. B. Flowers, *Toward Benevolent Neutrality: Church, State and the Supreme Court* (Markham, 1977); Wilbur G. Katz, *Religion and American Constitutions* (Northwestern University Press, 1964); and Philip B. Kurland, *Religion and the Law: Of Church and State and the Supreme Court* (Aldine Publishing Co., 1962). Richard E. Morgan's *The Politics of Religious Conflict: Church and State in America,* 2d ed. (University Press of America, 1980), posits some intriguingly unorthodox suggestions. Interesting case studies are Theodore Powell, *The School Bus Law: A Case Study in Education, Religion, and Politics* (Wesleyan University Press, 1960); Albert N. Keim, *Compulsory Education and the Amish: The Right Not To Be Modern* (Beacon Press, 1975); E. F. Frazier, *The Negro Church in America* (Schocken, 1969); and Victor E. Blackwell, *O'er The Ramparts They Watched* (Carlton, 1976), a work by one of the leading attorneys for the Jehovah's Witnesses. The best historical work extant on the controversial problem of the free exercise of religion and conscientious objection is still Mulford Q. Sibley and Philip E. Jacob, *Conscription of Conscience: The American State and the Conscientious Objector, 1940–1947* (Cornell University Press, 1952), though it must now be supplemented with readings of recent significant Supreme Court decisions, such as *United States v. Seeger,* 380 U.S. 163 (1965); *Welsh v. United States,* 398 U.S. 333 (1970); and *Gillette v. United States* plus *Negre v. Larsen,* 401 U.S. 437 (1971). Also valuable is Milton R. Konvitz's *Religious Liberty and Conscience: A Constitutional Inquiry* (Viking, 1969). Gordon W. Allport's *The Individual and His Religion* (Macmillan, 1950), blends philosophical with pragmatic considerations; William H. Marnell's *The First Amendment: The History of Religious Freedom in America* (Doubleday, 1964), is a valuable account: and Davis R. Manwaring's *Render Unto Caesar: The Flag-Salute Controversy* (University of Chicago Press, 1962), gives us the exciting, engagingly written story of the *Flag Salute* cases of the early 1940s—cases that tell us much about line-drawing and the judicial process. The complete legal briefs, court proceedings, and decisions in the heart-rending, fascinating case of *Karen Ann Quinlan* are available in a handy publication by University Publishers of America, 1975.

Lastly, some suggested further readings on egalitarianism, on race and gender, especially the former. Gunnar Myrdal's epic *An American Dilemma: The Negro Problem and Modern Democracy,* rev. ed. (Harper, 1962), is still an essential introduction to the problem. C. Vann Woodward's informative and purposeful work, *The Strange Career of Jim Crow,* 3d ed. (Oxford University Press, 1974), explains definitively the origin and development of "Jim Crow." Loren Miller, son of a Negro slave and his white wife, has a highly useful work on the story of the Court and the Negro, *The Petitioners* (Pantheon Books, 1966). Betty Friedan's *The Feminine Mystique* (Norton, 1963) and Kate Millet's *Sexual Politics* (Doubleday, 1970) provided *the* literary impetus for the rising women's movement. A thorough overview of the latter's dénouement may be found in Leslie F. Goldstein's *The Constitutional Rights of Women: Cases in Law and Social Change* (Longman, 1979). Paul Lewinson's *Race, Class, and Party: A History of Negro Suffrage and White Politics in the South* (Russell and Russell, 1963), illustrates well the rocky road that led to the successful Voting Rights Act of 1965. To understand that other road, which—at least on paper—reached its destination faster by a decade, the road to the desegregated schoolhouse, one could do no better than to read some of the pertinent key Supreme Court decisions: *The Civil Rights Cases,* 109 U.S. 3 (1883); *Plessy v. Ferguson,* 163 U.S. 537 (1896), which made "separate but equal" king for almost six decades; *Missouri ex rel. Gaines v. Canada,* 305 U.S. 337 (1938); *Sweatt v. Painter,* 339 U.S. 629 (1950); and, of course, the *Public School Desegregation Cases* of 1954 and 1955 (see Chapter VII), which heralded the death of "separate but equal"—not only in education but elsewhere. A handy and factual description of the last decisions is Daniel M. Berman's *It Is So Ordered: The Supreme Court Rules on School Segregation* (Norton, 1966); but the best work to date on *Brown* is Richard Kluger's mammoth *Simple Justice: The History of Brown v. Board of Education and Black America's Struggle for Equality* (Knopf, 1975). Literally thousands of books have appeared on the subject of race; among those that stand out are J. Harvie Wilkinson III's ably analytical and historical *From Brown to Bakke* (Oxford University Press, 1979); Walter Lord's *The Past That Would Not Die* (Harper and Row, 1965); Robert J. Harris's eloquent activist plea, *The Quest for Equality: The Constitu-*

tion, Congress, and the Supreme Court (Louisiana State University Press, 1960); and Charles E. Silberman's *Crisis in Black and White* (Random House, 1964), an important analysis of fundamentals. Also outstanding are Lerone Bennett, Jr., *Confrontation: Black and White* (Penguin Books, 1966); James W. Silver's courageous analysis, *Mississippi: The Closed Society,* enl. ed. (Harcourt, Brace & World, 1966), which became a classic example of the basic problem that existed in certain areas of the deep South; Pat Watters's excellent analysis and exposition, *The South and the Nation* (Pantheon, 1970); the important statistical study by W. Brink and L. Harris, *Black and White: A Study of U.S. Racial Attitudes Today* (Simon & Schuster, 1967); and the sanguine tome by W. W. Wilson, *The Declining Significance of Race* (University of Chicago Press, 1978). The continuing emotion-charged issue of "affirmative action"—"reverse discrimination," highlighted by the non-decision in *De Funis v. Odegaard,* 417 U.S. 532 (1974), that of the "balancing" one of *Regents of the University of California v. Bakke,* 438 U.S. 265 (1978), and that of the perhaps most contentious one of *United Steelworkers v. Weber,* 442 U.S. 193 (1979), is the subject of an increasing number of works on what, together with forced busing, turned into the most volatile civil rights issue of the 1970s. Among them are: Nathan Glazer's pointed *Affirmative Discrimination* (Basic Books, 1976); Robert A. Rossum, *Reverse Discrimination: The Constitutional Debate* (Dekker, 1980); Robert M. O'Neill, *Discriminating Against Discrimination* (Indiana University Press, 1975); George Roche, *The Balancing Act: Quota Hiring in Higher Education* (Open Court, 1974); and Robert Dworkin, *Taking Rights Seriously* (Harvard University Press, 1977).

The volatile *busing* issue, dramatically brought to the fore in the seminal Supreme Court decision in *Swann v. Charlotte-Mecklenburg Board of Education,* 402 U.S. 1 (1971), has been addressed widely in the literature: e.g., L. Rubin's *Busing and Backlash* (University of California Press, 1972); Robert H. Bork, *Constitutionality of the President's Busing Proposals* (American Enterprise Institute, 1972); Nicolaus Mills (ed.), *The Great School Bus Controversy* (Texas Christian Press, 1973); James Bolner and Robert Shanley, *Busing: The Political and Judicial Process* (Praeger, 1974); "Busing—The Supreme Court Goes North," a prophetic article by Christopher Jencks, *The New York Times Magazine,* November 19, 1972, pp. 40 ff; and Linus A. Graglia's potent *Disaster by Decree: The Supreme Court Decisions on Race and the Schools* (Cornell University Press, 1976).

For works on the evolving techniques of the Negro civil rights movement, which have led to serious line-confrontations both in a physical and a legal sense, important treatises are: Estelle Fuchs, *Pickets at the Gates* (Free Press, 1966), which deals with difficulties inherent in the metropolis of New York City; W. Haywood Burns, *The Voices of Negro Protest in America* (Oxford University Press, 1963), an excellent historical and analytical study of Negro pressure groups, especially the Muslims; Everett C. Ladd, Jr., *Negro Political Leadership in the South* (Cornell University Press, 1966), an important analysis of an all-too-neglected aspect of the problem: Howard Zinn's description and evaluation of the "energetic young radicals" in *SNCC: The Abolitionists* (Beacon Press, 1964); Arthur I. Waskow's overview, *From Race Riot to Sit-in:*

1919 and the 1960's (Doubleday, 1966); the intelligent political analysis of the rising influence of the Negro voter by Donald R. Matthews and James W. Prothro, *Negroes and the New Southern Politics* (Harcourt, Brace & World, 1966); P. S. Foner's study of the increasingly visible Black Panthers, *The Black Panthers Speak* (Lippincott, 1970); Martin Oppenheimer's *The Urban Guerilla* (Quadrangle, 1969); J. H. Cone's *Black Theology and Black Power* (Seabury Press, 1969); Thomas Wagstaff's *Black Power: The Radical Response to White America* (The Glencoe Press, 1969); Alan Altshuler's *Community Control: The Black Demand for Participation in Large American Cities* (Pegasus, 1970); the influential Saul Alinsky's *Rules for Radicals: A Pragmatic Primer for Realistic Radicals* (Random House, 1971); W. D. Wynn's *The Black Protest Movement* (Philosophical Library, 1974); E. Patterson's *Black City Politics* (Dodd, Mead, 1975); and W. H. Chafe's *Civilities and Civil Rights: Greensboro, North Carolina, and the Black Struggle for Freedom* (Oxford University Press, 1980).

Finally in this brief bibliography, the vexatious "state action" problem, which has dominated so many facets of the race issue, is discussed in several excellent works. Among them are Paul G. Kauper's penetrating chapter "Private and Governmental Actions: Fluid Concepts," in his *Civil Liberties and the Constitution* (University of Michigan Press, 1962); Jerre Williams's "Twilight of State Action," 4 *Texas Law Review* 374 (February 1963); the already listed book by Robert J. Harris; and Morrow Berger's *Equality by Statute: The Revolution in Civil Rights,* rev. ed. (Doubleday, 1967). Among several, two distinguished scholars have raised basic issues of the state action problem that will probably always be with us in some form even though the legislative and judicial processes have to some extent passed them by: Herbert Wechsler, "Toward Neutral Principles of Constitutional Law," 73 *Harvard Law Review* 1, which appeared in November 1959 and is still widely discussed; and Louis Henkin, "Shelley v. Kraemer: Notes for a Revised Opinion," 110 *University of Pennsylvania Law Review* 473 (February 1962), a searching, troubled, and honest essay. A host of fascinating cases involving the state-action/private-action dichotomy point to what will indubitably be a continuing source of constitutional controversy—among them: *Reitman v. Mulkey,* 387 U.S. 369 (1967), the California Fair Housing Ban Proposition Case; *Jones v. Alfred H. Mayer Co.,* 392 U.S. 409 (1968), the first contemporary Civil Rights Act of *1866* case; *Palmer v. Thompson,* 403 U.S. 217 (1971), the Mississippi Pool Closing case; *Moose Lodge #107 v. Irvis,* 407 U.S. 163 (1972), the Private Club Ban of Blacks case; *Tillman v. Wheaton-Haven Recreation Association,* 410 U.S. 431 (1973), the Montgomery County, Maryland, Swimming Facilities case; and, perhaps most contentiously, *Runyon v. McCrary,* 427 U.S. 160, the 1976 Virginia Private School Segregation case.

It would be easy to continue—but here too, lines must be drawn.

Appendix A

STATISTICAL DATA ON SUPREME COURT JUSTICES

APPOINTING PRESIDENT	DATES OF PRESIDENT'S SERVICE	PRESIDENT'S POLITICAL PARTY	NAME OF JUSTICE	DATES OF BIRTH & DEATH	JUSTICE'S NOMINAL PARTY ALLEGIANCE ON APPOINTMENT	STATE FROM WHICH JUSTICE WAS APPTD.#	DATES OF SERVICE ON SUPREME COURT
Washington	1789–1797	Federalist	1. Jay, John*	1745–1829	Federalist	N.Y.	1789–1795
"			2. Rutledge, John	1739–1800	"	S.C.	1789–1791†
"			3. Cushing, William	1732–1810	"	Mass.	1789–1810
"			4. Wilson, James	1724–1798	"	Pa.	1789–1798
"			5. Blair, John	1732–1800	"	Va.	1789–1796
"			6. Iredell, James	1750–1799	"	N.C.	1790–1799
"			7. Johnson, Thomas	1732–1819	"	Md.	1791–1793
"			8. Paterson, Wm.	1745–1806	"	N.J.	1793–1806
"			9. Rutledge, John*	1739–1800	"	S.C.	1796‡
"			10. Chase, Samuel	1741–1811	"	Md.	1796–1811
Adams	1797–1801	"	11. Ellsworth, Oliver*	1745–1807	"	Conn.	1796–1800
"			12. Washington, Bushrod	1762–1829	"	Va.	1798–1829
"			13. Moore, Alfred	1755–1810	"	N.C.	1799–1804
"			14. Marshall, John*	1755–1835	"	Va.	1801–1835
Jefferson	1801–1809	Republican	15. Johnson, Wm.	1771–1834	Republican	S.C.	1804–1834
"			16. Livingston, Brockholst	1757–1823	"	N.Y.	1806–1823
"			17. Todd, Thomas	1765–1826	"	Ky.	1807–1826
Madison	1809–1817	"	18. Duval, Gabriel	1752–1844	"	Md.	1811–1835
"			19. Story, Joseph	1779–1845	"	Mass.	1811–1845
Monroe	1817–1825	"	20. Thompson, Smith	1768–1843	"	N.Y.	1823–1843
Adams	1825–1829	"	21. Trimble, Robert	1777–1828	"	Ky.	1826–1828
Jackson	1829–1837	Democrat	22. McLean, John	1785–1861	Democrat	Ohio	1829–1861
"			23. Baldwin, Henry	1780–1844	"	Pa.	1830–1844
"			24. Wayne, James M.	1790–1867	"	Ga.	1835–1867

* Chief Justice. † Resigned without sitting.
‡ Unconfirmed recess appointment, rejected by Senate, Dec. 1795.
# Not necessarily, but often, state of birth.

STATISTICAL DATA ON SUPREME COURT JUSTICES—Continued

APPOINTING PRESIDENT	PRESIDENT'S POLITICAL PARTY	DATES OF PRESIDENT'S SERVICE	NAME OF JUSTICE	DATES OF BIRTH & DEATH	JUSTICE'S NOMINAL PARTY ALLEGIANCE ON APPOINTMENT	STATE FROM WHICH JUSTICE WAS APPTD.#	DATES OF SERVICE ON SUPREME COURT
"	"	"	25. Taney, Roger B.*	1777–1864	"	Md.	1836–1864
"	"	"	26. Barbour, Philip P.	1783–1841	"	Va.	1836–1841
"	"	"	27. Catron, John§	1778–1865	"	Tenn.	1837–1865
Van Buren	"	1837–1841	28. McKinley, John	1780–1852	"	Ala.	1837–1852
"	"	"	29. Daniel, Peter V.	1784–1860	"	Va.	1841–1860
Tyler	Whig	1841–1845	30. Nelson, Samuel	1792–1873	"	N.Y.	1845–1872
Polk	Democrat	1845–1849	31. Woodbury, Levi	1789–1851	"	N.H.	1845–1851
"	"	"	32. Grier, Robert C.	1794–1870	"	Pa.	1846–1870
Fillmore	Whig	1850–1853	33. Curtis, Benjamin R.	1809–1874	Whig	Mass.	1851–1857
Pierce	Democrat	1853–1857	34. Campbell, John A.	1811–1889	Democrat	Ala.	1853–1861
Buchanan	Democrat	1857–1861	35. Clifford, Nathan	1803–1881	"	Me.	1858–1881
Lincoln	Republican	1861–1865	36. Swayne, Noah H.	1804–1884	Republican	Ohio	1862–1881
"	"	"	37. Miller, Samuel F.	1816–1890	"	Iowa	1862–1890
"	"	"	38. Davis, David	1815–1886	"	Ill.	1862–1877
"	"	"	39. Field, Stephen J.	1816–1899	Democrat	Cal.	1863–1897
"	"	"	40. Chase, Salmon P.*	1808–1873	Republican	Ohio	1864–1873
Grant	"	1869–1877	41. Strong, William	1808–1895	"	Pa.	1870–1880
"	"	"	42. Bradley, Joseph P.	1803–1892	"	N.J.	1870–1892
"	"	"	43. Hunt, Ward	1810–1886	"	N.Y.	1872–1882
"	"	"	44. Waite, Morrison R.*	1816–1888	"	Ohio	1874–1888
Hayes	"	1877–1881	45. Harlan, John M.	1833–1911	"	Ky.	1877–1911
"	"	"	46. Woods, William B.	1824–1887	"	Ga.	1880–1887
Garfield	"	Mar.–Sept.	47. Matthews, Stanley	1824–1889	"	Ohio	1881–1889
Arthur	"	1881–1885	48. Gray, Horace	1828–1902	"	Mass.	1881–1902
"	"	"	49. Blatchford, Samuel	1820–1893	"	N.Y.	1882–1893
Cleveland	Democrat	1885–1889	50. Lamar, Lucius Q. C.	1825–1893	Democrat	Miss.	1888–1893
"	"	"	51. Fuller, Melville*	1833–1910	"	Ill.	1888–1910

414

President	Party	Term	#	Justice	Dates	Party	State#	Term
Harrison	Republican	1889–1893	52.	Brewer, David J.	1837–1910	Republican	Kans.	1889–1910
"	"	"	53.	Brown, Henry B.	1836–1913	"	Mich.	1890–1906
"	"	"	54.	Shiras, George, Jr.	1832–1924	"	Pa.	1892–1903
Cleveland	Democrat	1893–1897	55.	Jackson, Howell E.	1832–1895	Democrat	Tenn.	1893–1895
"	"	"	56.	White, Edward D.	1854–1921	"	La.	1894–1910
"	"	"	57.	Peckham, Rufus W.	1838–1909	"	N.Y.	1895–1909
McKinley	Republican	1897–1901	58.	McKenna, Joseph	1843–1926	Republican	Cal.	1898–1925
Roosevelt	Republican	1901–1909	59.	Holmes, Oliver W., Jr.	1841–1935	"	Mass.	1902–1932
"	"	"	60.	Day, William R.	1849–1923	"	Ohio	1903–1922
"	"	"	61.	Moody, William H.	1853–1917	"	Mass.	1906–1910
Taft	Republican	1909–1913	62.	Lurton, Horace	1844–1914	Democrat	Tenn.	1909–1914
"	"	"	63.	Hughes, Charles E.	1862–1948	Republican	N.Y.	1910–1916
"	"	"	64.	White, Edward D.†*	1845–1921	Democrat	La.	1910–1921
"	"	"	65.	Van Devanter, Willis	1859–1941	Republican	Wyo.	1910–1937
"	"	"	66.	Lamar, Joseph R.	1857–1916	Democrat	Ga.	1910–1916
"	"	"	67.	Pitney, Mahlon	1858–1924	Republican	N.J.	1912–1922
Wilson	Democrat	1913–1921	68.	McReynolds, J. C.	1862–1946	Democrat	Tenn.	1914–1941
"	"	"	69.	Brandeis, Louis D.	1856–1941	Republican‡	Mass.	1916–1939
"	"	"	70.	Clarke, John H.	1857–1945	Democrat	Ohio	1916–1922
Harding	Republican	1921–1923	71.	Taft, William H.*	1857–1930	Republican	Conn.	1921–1930
"	"	"	72.	Sutherland, George	1862–1942	"	Utah	1922–1938
"	"	"	73.	Butler, Pierce	1866–1939	Democrat	Minn.	1922–1939
"	"	"	74.	Sanford, Edward T.	1865–1930	Republican	Tenn.	1923–1930
Coolidge	Republican	1923–1929	75.	Stone, Harlan F.	1872–1946	"	N.Y.	1925–1941
Hoover	Republican	1923–1933	76.	Hughes, Charles E.*	1862–1948	"	N.Y.	1930–1941
"	"	"	77.	Roberts, Owen J.	1875–1955	"	Pa.	1930–1945
"	"	"	78.	Cardozo, Benjamin	1870–1938	Democrat	N.Y.	1932–1938
Roosevelt	Democrat	1933–1945	79.	Black, Hugo L.	1886–1971	"	Ala.	1937–1971
"	"	"	80.	Reed, Stanley F.	1884–1980	"	Ky.	1938–1957
"	"	"	81.	Frankfurter, Felix	1883–1965	Independent	Mass.	1939–1962
"	"	"	82.	Douglas, William	1898–1980	Democrat	Conn.	1939–1975

* Chief Justice.   † Promoted from Associate Justice.

‡ Many—and with some justice—consider Brandeis a Democrat; however, he was in fact a registered Republican when nominated.

Not necessarily, but often, state of birth.

§ Catron was nominated by Jackson but he was not confirmed until Van Buren had assumed the presidency.

STATISTICAL DATA ON SUPREME COURT JUSTICES—Continued

APPOINTING PRESIDENT	PRESIDENT'S POLITICAL PARTY	DATES OF PRESIDENT'S SERVICE	NAME OF JUSTICE	DATES OF BIRTH & DEATH	JUSTICE'S NOMINAL PARTY ALLEGIANCE ON APPOINTMENT	STATE FROM WHICH JUSTICE WAS APPTD.#	DATES OF SERVICE ON SUPREME COURT
"	"	"	83. Murphy, Frank	1893–1949	"	Mich.	1940–1949
"	"	"	84. Byrnes, James F.	1879–1972	"	S.C.	1941–1942
"	"	"	85. Stone, Harlan F.†*	1872–1946	Republican	N.Y.	1941–1946
"	"	"	86. Jackson, Robert H.	1892–1954	Democrat	N.Y.	1941–1954
"	"	"	87. Rutledge, Wiley B.	1894–1949	"	Iowa	1943–1949
Truman	"	1945–1953	88. Burton, Harold H.	1888–1965	Republican	Ohio	1945–1958
"	"	"	89. Vinson, Fred M.*	1890–1953	Democrat	Ky.	1946–1953
"	"	"	90. Clark, Tom C.	1899–1977	"	Tex.	1949–1967
"	"	"	91. Minton, Sherman	1890–1965	"	Ind.	1949–1956
Eisenhower	Republican	1953–1961	92. Warren, Earl*	1891–1974	Republican	Cal.	1953–1969
"	"	"	93. Harlan, John M., Jr.	1899–1971	"	N.Y.	1955–1971
"	"	"	94. Brennan, Wm. J.	1906–	Democrat	N.J.	1956–
"	"	"	95. Whittaker, Charles	1900–1973	Republican	Mo.	1957–1962
"	"	"	96. Stewart, Potter	1915–	"	Ohio	1958–1981
Kennedy	Democrat	1961–1963	97. White, Byron R.	1917–	Democrat	Colo.	1962–
"	"	"	98. Goldberg, Arthur	1908–	"	Ill.	1962–1965
Johnson	"	1963–1969	99. Fortas, Abe	1910–	"	Tenn.	1965–1969
"	"	"	100. Marshall, Thurgood	1910–	"	N.Y.	1967–
Nixon	Republican	1969–1974	101. Burger, Warren E.*	1907–	Republican	Va.	1969–
"	"	"	102. Blackmun, Harry A.	1908–	"	Minn.	1970–
"	"	"	103. Powell, Lewis F., Jr.	1907–	Democrat	Va.	1972–
"	"	"	104. Rehnquist, William H.	1924–	Republican	Ariz.	1972–
Ford	"	1974–1977	105. Stevens, John Paul	1920–	"	Ill.	1975–
Reagan	Republican	1981–	106. O'Connor, Sandra D.	1930–	Republican	Ariz.	1981–

* Chief Justice.   † Promoted from Associate Justice.
# Not necessarily, but often, state of birth.

416

Appendix B. Civil Rights and Liberties in the Constitution

First Ten Amendments (*Adopted in 1791*)

AMENDMENT I

Congress shall make no law respecting an establishment of religion, or prohibiting the free exercise thereof; or abridging the freedom of speech, or of the press; or the right of the people peaceably to assemble and to petition the Government for a redress of grievances.

AMENDMENT II

A well-regulated militia being necessary to the security of a free State, the right of the people to keep and bear arms, shall not be infringed.

AMENDMENT III

No soldier shall, in time of peace, be quartered in any house without the consent of the owner, nor in time of war but in a manner to be proscribed by law.

AMENDMENT IV

The right of the people to be secure in their persons, houses, papers, and effects, against unreasonable searches and seizures, shall not be violated, and no warrants shall issue but upon probable cause, supported by oath or affirmation, and particularly describing the place to be searched, and the persons or things to be seized.

AMENDMENT V

No person shall be held to answer for a capital, or otherwise infamous crime, unless on a presentment or indictment of a Grand Jury, except in cases arising in the land or naval forces, or in the militia, when in actual service in time of war or public danger; nor shall any person be subject for the same offense to be twice put in jeopardy of life or limb; nor shall be compelled in any criminal case to be a witness against himself, nor be deprived of life, liberty or property, without due process of law; nor shall private property be taken for public use, without just compensation.

Amendment VI

In all criminal prosecutions, the accused shall enjoy the right to a speedy and public trial, by an impartial jury of the State and district wherein the crime shall have been committed, which districts shall have been previously ascertained by law, and to be informed of the nature and cause of the accusation; to be confronted with the witnesses against him; to have compulsory process for obtaining witnesses in his favor, and to have the assistance of counsel for his defense.

Amendment VII

In suits at common law, where the value in controversy shall exceed twenty dollars, the right of trial by jury shall be preserved, and no fact tried by a jury, shall be otherwise re-examined in any court of the United States, than according to the rules of the common law.

Amendment VIII

Excessive bail shall not be required, nor excessive fines imposed, nor cruel and unusual punishments inflicted.

Amendment IX

The enumeration in the Constitution of certain rights shall not be construed to deny or disparage others retained by the people.

Amendment X

The powers not delegated to the United States by the Constitution, nor prohibited by it to the States, are reserved to the States respectively, or to the people.

Other Amendments

Amendment XIII   (Ratified in 1865)

Section 1. Neither slavery nor involuntary servitude, except as a punishment for crime whereof the party shall have been duly convicted, shall exist within the United States, or any place subject to their jurisdiction.

Section 2. Congress shall have power to enforce this article by appropriate legislation.

Amendment XIV   (Ratified in 1868)

Section 1. All persons born or naturalized in the United States, and subject to the jurisdiction thereof, are citizens of the United States and of the State wherein they reside. No State shall make or enforce any law which shall abridge the privileges or immunities of citizens of the United States; nor shall any State deprive any person of life, liberty, or property, without due process of law; nor deny to any person within its jurisdiction the equal protection of the laws. . . .

Section 5. The Congress shall have power to enforce by appropriate legislation the provisions of this article.

AMENDMENT XV   (Ratified in 1870)

Section 1. The right of citizens of the United States to vote shall not be denied or abridged by the United States or by any State on account of race, color, or previous condition of servitude.

Section 2. The Congress shall have power to enforce this article by appropriate legislation.

AMENDMENT XIX   (Ratified in 1920)

The right of citizens of the United States to vote shall not be denied or abridged by the United States or by any State on account of sex.

Congress shall have power to enforce this article by appropriate legislation.

AMENDMENT XXIV   (Ratified in 1964)

Section 1. The right of citizens of the United States to vote in any primary or other election for President or Vice-President, for electors for President or Vice-President, or for Senator or Representative in Congress, shall not be denied or abridged by the United States or any state by reason of failure to pay any poll tax or other tax.

Section 2. The Congress shall have power to enforce this article by appropriate legislation.

AMENDMENT XXVI   (Ratified 1971)

Section 1. The right of citizens of the United States, who are 18 years of age or older, to vote shall not be denied or abridged by the United States or by any State on account of age.

Section 2. The Congress shall have power to enforce this article by appropriate legislation.

PROPOSED AMENDMENT XXVII   (Proposed March 22, 1972)

Section 1. Equality of rights under the law shall not be denied or abridged by the United States or by any State on account of sex.

Section 2. The Congress shall have power to enforce, by appropriate legislation, the provisions of this article.

Section 3. This amendment shall take effect two years after date of ratification.

Provisions from the Original Constitution

ARTICLE I

Section 9. . . .

2. The privilege of the writ of habeas corpus shall not be suspended, unless when in cases of rebellion or invasion the public safety may require it.

3. No bill of attainder or ex post facto law shall be passed.

Section 10.

1. No State shall . . . pass any bill of attainder, ex post facto law, or law impairing the obligation of contracts. . . .

ARTICLE III
  Section 2. . . .
      3. The trial of all crimes, except in cases of impeachment, shall be by jury. . . .
  Section 3.
      1. Treason against the United States shall consist only in levying war against them, or in adhering to their enemies, giving them aid and comfort. No Person shall be convicted of treason unless on the testimony of two witnesses to the same overt act, or on confession in open court.

ARTICLE IV
  Section 2.
      1. The citizens of each State shall be entitled to all privileges and immunities of citizens in the several States.

ARTICLE VI
      3. . . . no religious test shall ever be required as a qualification to any office or public trust under the United States.

I. General Index

abortion, 7, 74
"Affirmative Action," 337ff., 365, 396
Alien and Sedition Acts (1798), 177
American Bar Association
report on Fair Trial and a Free Press, 165
American Jewish Congress
recommendations for constitutional test of Federal Aid to Education Act (1965), 302
Amicus curiae, brief, 66, 329
Anti-Ku Klux Klan Act (1871), 313
appeal, writ of, 6
Assize of Clarendon, 76
Awake!, 237

bad tendency test, 209–10. *See also* expression, freedom of
Gitlow v. New York, 209-12
bail, 83
basic freedoms
crucial nature of, 21–22
Bill for Establishing Religious Freedom (Disestablishment Bill), 259
Bill of Rights, 17, 21, 28–91, 221, 276. *See also enumerated amendments*
applicability to states, 28ff.
Barron v. Baltimore, 28–30
historical background, 28–29
Birmingham (Ala.), 368–69
Black Panthers, 366
"blue ribbon" jury, 134
Boston, 342
boycotting. *See* race
Brandeis brief, 9
British Privy Council, 6
Buffalo (N.Y.), 311
busing. *See* race

capital punishment, 64
carpetbagger, 42

Central Intelligence Agency, 169
certiorari, writ of, 6
Chambre de Droit Public of the *Tribunal Federal Suisse* (Switzerland), 191
Chicago (Ill.), 311
child benefit theory, 278, 295–96, 303
Christian Scientists, 252
citizenship
defined in *Slaughterhouse Cases,* 41
and the Fourteenth Amendment, 31
civil disobedience, 5
Civil Rights Act (1866), 349, 352, 384–86, 389–90
Civil Rights Act (1871), 7
Civil Rights Act (1875), 319–20
Civil Rights Act (1957), 317, 346–57, 352, 360
Civil Rights Act (1960), 347, 352, 357
Civil Rights Act (1964), 31, 252, 337, 339, 348–52, 360–61, 371–72, 377–78, 384, 386, 388, 392, 397, 399
Civil Rights Act (1966), 37, 351, 360, 370, 389
Civil Rights Act (1968), 351–52, 378, 386, 392
Civil Rights Division and Section of the Department of Justice, 316
Classification, 322
"clear and present danger" test, 52, 181, 204–9. *See also* expression, freedom of; incorporation of the Bill of Rights
Cleveland (Ohio), 311
Committee on Fair Employment Practices, 314–16
Committee on Government Contract Compliance, 316
Common Cause, 133
Communist Control Act (1954), 180
Congress on Racial Equality (CORE), 366–68, 378

II. Name Index

III. Court Cases Index

433